TRUE MAN
TRUE WAYS

A Roadmap of Discovery to the
Masculine Heart

MIKE VAN PELT

eBook ISBN: 978-1-965761-14-4
Paperback ISBN: 978-1-965761-15-1
Hardcover ISBN: 978-1-965761-17-5
Ingram Spark ISBN: 978-1-965761-16-8
Library of Congress Control Number: 2024924738

Spotlight Publishing House™, Goodyear, AZ
https://spotlightpublishinghouse.com

Editor: Bethany Good https://goodwritingco.com
Book Cover Image: Adobe Stock
Book Cover Design: Angie Ayala
Book Layout: Marigold2k

For More Information:
https://truemanlifecoaching.com
https://truemanpodcast.com/

TRUE MAN
TRUE WAYS

A Roadmap of Discovery to the
Masculine Heart

MIKE VAN PELT

SPOTLIGHT
PUBLISHING HOUSE

Goodyear, AZ

Table of Contents

Endorsements

"In *True Man — True Ways*, Mike shares his own journey that led him to explore the deeper questions of living life wholeheartedly. He discusses many of the false assumptions we live in and offers a more hopeful understanding of purposeful living within biblical masculinity. If you are a man that is wondering if there is truly "something more" available, this book is for you!"
— **Paul Baily**, AAMS® CKA®
Founder, Palmetto Private Wealth

"Mike Van Pelt's *True Man* is a powerful guide for men seeking authenticity, purpose, and a life of deeper connection. As a NeuroCoach, I resonate with his profound understanding of the inner journey, the significance of emotional well-being, and the call to redefine masculinity in today's world. His metaphor of the 'open road' elegantly mirrors the dynamic and evolving path of self-discovery. This book not only provides a roadmap for navigating challenges but also inspires a transformation of the heart and mind, aligning action with purpose. A must-read for any man ready to step into his full potential and leave a meaningful legacy."
— **Luc Cardinal**,
Creator of the Begotten Method and Neurocoach

"Men are in crisis. Addiction, loneliness, and suicides are rising, yet support for men has dwindled. In *True Man — True Ways*, Mike Van Pelt offers a healing roadmap, grounded in faith and the example of one of the greatest men in history — Jesus. For men who feel like Prodigal Sons, this book guides you back home. Its message is not about competition but a collaboration reminder that we are one family and, together, we can create

heaven on earth. If you or a man you know is struggling, this book is a lifeline."
— **Derek Rydall**,
Author, *Emergence* and *The Abundance*
http://www.DerekRydall.com

"Wow, if you are looking for a real Christ centered direction to take as a man, or if you are struggling to see yourself as a Christian man through God's eyes, True Man —True Ways is the book for you! Mike Van Pelt takes men on a journey of self-discovery through God's direction and purpose in and for their lives."
— **Chris Tice**
Vice President, Givers University® USA Sales & Growth

"*True Man — True Ways* is more than a book — it's a battle cry for men who are ready to reclaim their lives. With a bold blend of biblical truth and real-world insight, Mike Van Pelt calls men to rise above mediocrity and embrace the purpose they were made for. This isn't about quick fixes or shallow self-help; it's a deeply practical and spiritual guide for building a life of impact, integrity, and faith. If you're tired of just getting by and ready to become the man God designed you to be, this book is your roadmap."
— **Jim Britt,**
Cracking the Rich Code
http://JimBrittVentures.com

"As someone who spends much time helping men with their personal transformation, I found the book *True Man — True Ways: A Roadmap of Discovery to the Masculine Heart* to be an excellent and comprehensive guide to assisting men with their overall character development. Mike Van Pelt covers all the vital areas necessary in mapping out the pathway to achieving success in all areas of our lives. Many men will benefit from this book."
— **Eddie Capparucci**, Ph.D., LPC, C-SAS
Abundant Life Counseling

"Many men I talk to are dead men walking. The reasons vary, but living a life isolated from intimate friendships is one major factor. The greatest factor of all is choosing to walk through life without the love and guidance of the One that created men to begin with. In *True Man — True Ways*, author Mike Van Pelt thoughtfully and skillfully lays the groundwork and road map for men, any man, to wake up from the slumber of mediocrity and broken dreams and create a plan that hurtles him into a fulfilling new journey."
— **Clint Hatton**, Founder of BigBoldBrave and Author of *Big Bold Brave – How to Live Courageously in a Risky World.*

"If you are a man who feels that despite your hard-won wisdom and accomplishments there is still something missing, then you must read this book. Mike is sharing the wisdom of his own journey and that of many other high character individuals. As men, we can sometimes feel that we should have all the answer by the time we reach a certain age. Mike dispels that myth and offers encouraging insights into how you can be your own best True Man."
— **Greg Payne**, Author and host of *The Cool Grandpa Podcast*

"In an age of self-imposed fragility and isolation, Van Pelt provides men a way to break free. Faith, fellowship, mental toughness — he addresses these personal qualities of the True Man in straightforward fashion. Fidelity to oneself means fidelity to a brotherhood. Van Pelt has the answers to the vexing questions of loneliness and consequent — and inevitable — self-destruction."
— **Jeff Nelligan**, Author, *Four Lesson From My Three Sons, How You Can Raise Resilient Kids*

"Mike Van Pelt is an invaluable resource to men, in an era when men need all the help we can get. This book will help men get their lives on the track they want to be on, but also do it from a place of deep-heartedness and not simply obligation and responsibility.

With Mike's help, men can find what they're looking for out of life."
— **Don Ross**
Founder, Manhood Tribes

"Through powerful biblical wisdom and real-world experience, Mike is your trusted guide on your journey to a better life. You'll discover practical ways to strengthen your faith while taking charge of your relationships, health, and purpose. Whether you're feeling stuck or just ready for more, True Man True Ways offers clear, genuine advice for becoming the man you're meant to be. It's like having a wise friend in your corner, showing you step-by-step how to build a life that truly counts — all while keeping God at the center. Simple, straightforward, and transformative."
— **Randy Pryor,** Men's Relationship Coach, and author of S.O.S. Reconnect — *Helping Separated Husbands Reconnect With Their Wives — Even If She's DONE.* RandyPryor.com

"Men, this book is for US — all of us that have asked questions of ourselves, our Lord, our purpose and our destiny. Mike has a gift of connecting with men and talking to us on our terms and how we'd understand. Do yourself a favor and Read, Digest, Consume this content as it can and will, if you let it, change the trajectory of your life. God is after our hearts, Men, so we can fulfill the good He has for us. Let's not waste another day. Thanks, Mike, for bringing this work to life and giving us guys a roadmap leading to Jesus!"
— **Victor Straw**, Owner Victory Driven LLC

"True Man — True Ways, is a powerful and thought-provoking guide for men looking to embrace true masculinity and faith. With heartfelt insights, Mike leads readers on a journey of self-discovery and resilience, inviting them to define their own path as a "True Man." Through personal stories, vivid metaphors, and a Christian perspective, this book addresses the struggles men face, from loneliness to finding purpose, and offers a roadmap to navigate life's complexities with strength, grace, and faith. This book is a call to build authentic brotherhood, find deeper connections, and live a legacy rooted in God's word."
— **Dr. Ed Slover**, President & Founder of Quest Consulting Service, LLC

"True Man is a refreshing, heartfelt roadmap that tackles what so many men are silently struggling with — living authentically beyond society's constraints. Mike Van Pelt offers men a path to redefine masculinity with purpose, faith, and resilience. It's a guide for any man who feels there's more to life than what he's been told — packed with wisdom for those ready to find their true selves."
— **Jarie Bolander**, author of *Ride or Die: Loving through Tragedy, a Husband's Memoir*

Dedication

To Jill:
No one has seen me live out this book more than you. It hasn't always been easy, but it's been sweet. You are everything I prayed for and everything I need. Thank you for all your love and support. I love you.

To Abbie and Zach:
I thank God daily He blessed me with you two. I hope and pray that I have been the father you always wanted and the True Man you need.

Mom and Dad:
Thank you for dragging me to church. I know it wasn't always easy, but look at it this way, your son is an author.

To Paul Baily and our Friday True Man Group:
Paul, thank you for the road trips and for instigating a Friday morning group. It's an honor to do life with you.

Thanks to the men who forged our True Man group on Friday mornings. Look, guys, I wrote a book.

Countless people have been part of my journey, each leaving a mark on the man I am today. Looking back, it's incredible to see how far I've come and to recognize those who helped shape me into the True Man I strive to be. You know who you are — God Bless and thank you.

Foreword

I met Mike in the Spring of 2019. He was taking a courageous step into one of our weekend conferences, intent on going deep with God and his own story. For the past 15 years I have had the privilege, honor, and frankly... challenge of working with men from all over the world, encouraging them to become more and more of *who they are* in the Kingdom. That always means shedding *who they aren't.*

Mike took the opportunity seriously that weekend and after, he kept going and we became friends.

For a man, writing a book is very much like painting a land-scape or writing a song. These are ventures that require an Artist, someone who is able to take their subject in, hold it close, then present it back to the world in a book, painting, or music that is a deeply personal expression of their heart.

How vulnerable.

How courageous.

In writing *True Man - True Ways,* Mike Van Pelt is both.

Most of us remember maps. The old school kind from Rand McNally. Before our phones did all the work for us, even before MapQuest. A time when you would "open" the multi-folded ginor-mous paper, (never to be able to fold it back correctly) and then read it. It is a given, step one: Identify where you are on the map and step two: locate where it is you want to go. Sounds pretty simple... but reading these type maps require something more, looking down and then looking up. Mike's book is the same, look down — *inward* — to see where you are and look up — *outward* — to see where God is.

About Traveling. There are always several ways to get somewhere. The scenic route, the fastest route, the route that allows you to see the biggest ball of twine in the world or the route that allows you to see a dear friend or a family member. So many ways to travel.

In his book, *True Man — True Ways*, Mike takes on the role of guide, this is a great way to travel, and gives his readers all the above, the scenic route with beautiful landscapes, strategic off the beaten path waypoints, hikes that take you to views from elevation in which to best see your life and the Life God is offering. In journeying through the pages of *True Man — True Ways* I believe it's going to be best for to stop, be still, and take it all in.

What an honor to see Mike explore, learn, and take notes these past several years and come to the place that what he has discovered as true, and helpful, and encouraging, has all inspired him to write it down so that other men might take their next steps on their masculine journey. Through personal stories, scripture, and the sharing of perspectives from other faith guides in his life, Mike offers practical steps for his readers to take in order that they might experience what Mike has experienced, the goodness of God in his life journey.

There is a lot in these pages, and it is my prayer that as you journey through them, the old man will fall away, and the True Man will emerge.

When we know someone is going to take to the road, we often say, "safe travels." With *True Man — True Ways*, I think I would rather say to you," God's Speed" because if I've learned one thing in walking with Mike these past years, this book is not safe, rather it is the narrow road, a path into and through the wild, and certainly this book is good.

God Speed,

—**Michael Thompson**, Zoweh Founder and President, Conference Speaker and Guide to men, and Author of *The Heart of a Warrior,* and *King Me.*
Durham/Chapel-Hill NC, 2025

Introduction

True Man True Ways,
A Roadmap of Discovery to the Masculine Heart

I'm writing this book because I see a landscape of lost masculine souls searching, questioning, and wondering if the guy to their right or left is struggling with some of the same questions. I have news for you: chances are they are wrestling with the same problems. Just know that you are not alone.

I've found it easy to question what the "church" has or hasn't done for lost hearts and masculine souls, but ultimately, that doesn't do much good. I wrote this book, I do my podcast, and I'm a men's life coach for one specific reason: I want men to experience more in their lives. I want men to be their best for the families they lead, and guess what? Your family, your wife, and those around you also want that for you. They want to see you grow and blossom into the man you were created to be.

Hence, this book is a roadmap back to your heart.

You remember maps, don't you? Those fold-up maps that took up space in the glove box of your car. How about an atlas? My dad still loves to pull that bad boy out and look where everything is located. Roadmaps provide you with a snapshot to go by and guide you on how to get from point A to point B. Nowadays, the GPS on your phone has taken over how we get anywhere. That said, a roadmap can help you get where you want to go, and in life, it can offer an on-ramp to success.

I've created *"True Man, True Ways: A Roadmap of Discovery, Back to the Masculine Heart"* because it hits me where I am now, and I don't think I'm alone. As I've been on my entrepreneurial journey, many people have asked, "What are your plans, strategy, and purpose?" "Who do you help?" and "How do you help them?" This book summarizes some of that, at least at this moment. I still consider myself on the path to becoming the man I want to become. What will this roadmap look like in 5, 10, or 20 years later? Chances are it will be repaved, reworked, and redeveloped, but I know the construction journey will be good under the care of an intimate relationship with God.

We're all under construction, all under development, and I think that's what this book is about. Can you be 1% better tomorrow than you were today? I hope the answer to that question is yes. My goal is to provide a roadmap of hope back to your heart on your masculine journey. As you will read, the road to a True Man is the path walked by Jesus Christ, which has created an intense curiosity in my life. How do I become a True Man? What is a True Man, and what does it take to be one? In this book, I provide you with basic steps on how to define what a True Man looks like for you.

Regardless of my disconnect with how to spell or the English language, I now find myself on a mission, and my sense of purpose is pushing me outside my comfort zone to pull together well-crafted sentences with all the words spelled correctly.

This mission isn't so much about writing as it is about how the words on a page can help a man change his thinking and being. You may be wondering why this is even important to me. It's a good question, and I hope the pages of this book will help you explore, through my experience and anecdotal stories, how to feel alive in your walk with God. Ultimately, I want to give you a roadmap toward your legacy and the hope that you can achieve your dreams. Am I a pastor or social worker? No. Am I a psychologist or a tenured professor? Not by a long shot. I am just like the everyday guy, the average "Joe" dude who found his soul while searching, digging, and barely breathing at certain points. I'm your neighbor, friend, and fellow church parishioner who walked around in a daze, wondering, "Is there more to life than this?"

Am I alone in asking this question? I have talked with, been exposed to, and seen men with the glossy look that said, "Am I built for this?" This has led me to believe that I'm not alone in wondering if I'm the man I want to be, or the man others want me to be.

In writing this book, I hope that I can inspire other men to begin to ask deeper questions, explore more, and give their fear to God. Is that an easy task? No. I know I've fought these questions, and worse than that, I thought someone other than God might show up with the answer.

Men, I know you're searching and wondering, and I guess some of you have almost given up the fight. While all of this is going on inside you, everything appears to be in order on the outside: the car, the house, the marriage, the children, and so on. But it's an unsustainable model built on the false self and a false identity.

Let's get real, men. There is a quiet desperation that goes on inside us, but exploring that may cause weakness to show up, and we wouldn't want to compromise our masculine selves, now, would we?

It's time to heal the wound, and we must start showing up as men, fathers, and spouses. I'm not writing to point fingers; at times, more times than I care to count, I've failed in all these areas.

How do we survive? How do we move on? How do we get better? These are valid questions; let's explore with our arms locked together as brothers who want a deeper, more meaningful relationship in Christ.

Today is the day, men. Let us encourage, love, and move towards a brotherhood of hope, joy, and intimacy. Let's be the men, fathers, husbands, and friends we were called to be. Let's be men for each other as brothers in Christ.

> *"For as the body is one, and hath many members, and all the members of that one body, being many, are one body: so, also is Christ. For by one Spirit are we all baptized into one body, whether we be Jews or Gentiles, whether we be bond or free; and have been all made to drink into one Spirit. For the body is not one member, but many."*
> 1 Corinthians 12:14

I'm praying you find what you're looking for in your journey to have more intimacy with Christ and enjoy the freedom that comes with it.

Mike Van Pelt

Warm Up the Engine For Our Road Trip!

Let's talk about road trips. First things first, make a checklist. Grab your license, registration, and insurance info — can't leave home without 'em. Stock up on snacks, water, and a first aid kit for emergencies. Don't be caught without chargers for your gadgets, a map or GPS, and any meds you might need. Pack clothes for the weather, comfy shoes, and something to keep you entertained.

Now, onto the car. Get that car serviced, the oil changed, filters checked, and fluids topped up. Give those hoses and belts a once-over, and don't slack on the tires — pressure and tread need to be solid. Oh, and brakes and battery — make sure they're good to go. And hey, don't forget to load up your favorite podcasts (I recommend the True Man Podcast) and tunes. Gas tank full? Is the owner's manual within reach?

Last but not least, have a plan. GPS on point? Know where you're headed and how to get there? Remember, if you're unsure of your destination, any road will get you nowhere fast. So, buckle up, check your mirrors, and let's hit the road, my friend.

Planning your life is a bit like gearing up for a road trip. You need to have a clear destination in mind, whether it's a specific career goal, a personal milestone, or a dream you're chasing. Just like plotting out your route on a map, you need to map out your goals and the steps to get there.

Along the way, you'll encounter obstacles and challenges, much like roadblocks and detours on a journey. But with careful planning and preparation, you can navigate through them and stay on course. And just like you wouldn't hit the road without a spare tire or emergency kit, it's important to have backup plans and support systems in place for when things don't go as expected. So, whether you're embarking on a literal road trip or mapping out your life's journey, remember to plan ahead, stay focused on your destination, and be prepared for whatever comes your way.

Here we go…

I don't think there's any doubt about it; men today are searching, busy, full of fear and doubt, running from place to place and wondering how to pull it all off. Over the years, dozens of people have told me, "Mike, you need to have a plan." This advice makes sense, but I'm not sure I ever fully understood how to put it into practice. And, yes, I've done that. I've stuck with a plan; I've tried to create goals and attain them, and guess what? Most of the time, it works. But the rest of the time, I forget about it. If we're all being honest with each other, as we should, the truth is that we're all guilty of getting sidetracked at some point. It happens. In life, it's hard to stay consistent because something always comes up, and you have to put it off for another time. At least that's what we tell ourselves.

It's easy to get wrapped up in the things happening around us and forget about what matters most.

My goal in this book is to give you a road map to help you navigate life's challenges and provide you with some rest stops. Of course, having directions, a map, GPS, and a way to get to where you're going are important. Knowing and planning your route to get to where you want to go when you're on a trip is important, but sometimes, what we miss along our journey are the rest stops to replenish our souls.

What I hope to provide you with in this book are rest stops — the oasis — to pause, to rest, to replenish, and to provide you with the attributes to get you where you want to go. The journey is valuable, but the rest stops are just as crucial. I hope this book will be an oasis for you along your journey.

Is there a right or wrong way to get where you want to go? Probably not, but here is my encouragement: have a wingman to help you along the way. Find a buddy, a mentor, or anyone to help you through the journey. I am not saying that you need someone to hold your hand and do everything for you but having someone who can help support and guide you in the right direction is very vital.

A critical part of this journey is having someone who will hold you accountable for your actions, help you find your way around the obstacles, and encourage you through the difficult times. You want someone willing to fight for your heart while you help them fight for theirs.

My wingman and copilot was Paul Bailey. The wonderful car trips we took together were a part of our journey. Quite often, a call for a cup of coffee entailed hopping in the car and marching from South Carolina up to the North Carolina border. Were there coffee shops in Spartanburg, South Carolina? The answer is yes, but the road trip was far more valuable than the coffee. The conversations we had, the opportunity to do life one-on-one, learn from each other, and help each other be better men for our families were really the secret sauce of a good, old-fashioned road trip.

Those trips to Open Road Coffee Roastery in Columbus, North Carolina, offered us a coffee oasis of sorts that allowed us to pause, ponder, and talk about our lives so that we could grow and become the men God has called us to be.

There's nothing revolutionary about hopping in the car and going for coffee with a good friend. The challenge is that many of us don't take the time to do it. Many of us don't take the time for soul care, for doing life together, or for being in the community. In fact, many of the men I meet are really searching for a fast-food Jesus in this fast-food world. We often want a quick fix, and many are bound and determined to find it. In a world of speed and attention spans that last five seconds, we seem to have lost the ability to follow the road that Jesus traveled — one of patience, perseverance, and love.

Speaking of speed and trips of sorts. I love Indianapolis-style race cars — the speed, the smell of the oil and tires, the adrenaline rush when the cars go by, and the power of hearing those engines. Anyone who knows me understands that the last Sunday in May, when the Indy 500 is run, is circled on my calendar. It's simply one of the best days of the year for me.

One year, for my birthday, my wife bought me an opportunity to participate in the Mario Andretti Racing Experience at Charlotte Motor Speedway in Charlotte, North Carolina. We had the chance to strap ourselves into one of those beautiful cars and hit the speedway for an Indy-style fast laps.

As the crew chief gave us the instructions, I wondered what I had gotten myself into. "Okay folks, there are two tracks on this speedway, one for you amateurs," he said dryly. I figured he must have given the same speech hundreds of times. "The outside line is for John over there. Now, John is a professional racer, and he'll be going at least 40 mph faster than you, so keep an eye on the way he moves. You gotta' maintain your line so you don't get in his way." You know that feeling of fear and anxiety that grips you when you're doing something exciting you've never done before? Let me just say it's exhilarating when someone passes you at almost 200 mph.

I was nervous and excited about getting in the car, but I followed the guide's instructions. I plugged in my earbuds so they could guide me around the track, put on my helmet, and strapped myself in. I remember sitting in the car and looking down pit road; all I could see was the wall outside, of turn one from the car. I remember thinking, "Holy cow, that wall looks really close." The next thing you know, they shoved me off, and I hit the gas.

It took me one and a half laps to get acclimated, whatever that means when you have a rocket ship underneath you. The most incredible thing occurred: I hit a top speed of 158 mph. This is certainly one of the most thrilling things I've ever done. The funny thing about it was that despite the speed, I felt like I was sitting still. I was ashamed to leave the car, thinking I hadn't gotten past 50 mph. Just so you know, they don't put speed gauges in the car; you really don't know how fast you're going. You can imagine my surprise when I hopped out of the car and discovered I had a fast lap of 158 mph.

Here are some takeaways from that thrilling day.

1. Push through fear. I was provided with clear directions, safety equipment, and a voice inside my ear guiding me around the track. God's word provides us with all of the direction and safety equipment we need in life. We only need to ask. He is our rock.
2. I love speed, but going fast is scary. Life is a lot like a race car; it's fast and scary, but whoever trusts in the Lord is safe.
3. Despite the excitement of the racing experience, it can be exhausting to focus on something so intently. Life leaves many men exhausted, frustrated, distracted, and worried that they won't be able to get to the finish line.

All the lessons from that day and what I've learned from life are why I put this book together. Trust me, as much as I enjoyed my ride at the track, making it back to the pit lanes in one piece really felt good.

The pits on a racetrack are cool, but the rest stop on the highway likely means you're on a road trip with your family or friends, and that's even cooler. Let's get the car warmed up and ready to go with some crucial information and directions for your trip. Then, I'll show you some great rest stops to learn, grow, and develop.

Ready? Buckle up! Let's go!

Chapter One

Identity:
The Backseat Driver
That Gets In Your Head

True Man Tip

Protect your personal identity like you would your personal information. Your authenticity is every bit as important to protect as your social security number. If you are not careful, it can be stolen as well.

Identity, Riding Shotgun

Have you ever found yourself questioning who you are? Do you wonder what's coming next in your life?

In the tangled maze of our lives, it's easy to lose sight of our identity. The quest to understand ourselves is a journey that resonates with every man. Join me as we embark on the first leg of our road trip in *"True Man True Ways, A Roadmap of Discovery to the Masculine Heart."* To start our trip, we're about to jump deep into the puzzling world of identity, a crucial aspect that forms the very foundation of your masculinity.

Hop in. Let's go for a drive on the road to discover your identity.

In this chapter, we're peeling back the layers to uncover the essence of your identity. We'll confront your internal challenges and unravel the complexities surrounding who you are. The roadmap ahead will guide you through a profound journey of self-discovery, setting the stage for the transformative journey that awaits you.

Addressing the pivotal question of identity isn't just about introspection; it's about shaping a life that aligns with your true self. This exploration is paramount — it's the key to unlocking your authentic masculinity and living a life that resonates with purpose and fulfillment.

When I think about identity, I think about time lost versus time gained. When we approach our lives with unrealistic expectations and without clearly defined goals, our time is lost. We are searching rather than forging ahead. Instead of planning, we fly by the seat of our pants. We are merely existing instead of truly living.

I remember getting my hands on my first fake ID. It almost felt like freedom knowing you could get through the bar doors and maybe even wrangle a 12-pack of beer from the grocery store.

What comes with all of that? Fear, anxiety, risk, stress, or panic, and none of these are good. If you could just enter the club door, you could finally become someone else at the bottom of a beer glass that didn't exist before.

The funny thing about identity is whether you know it or not, it's your truth. You can become what you want at the moment, but if you're not careful, it can become an unfortunate and permanent part of your story.

If you ignore your truth, you can become someone that you don't even recognize. That man can find himself curled up in the fetal position in the corner of that bar, wondering who he is and how he got there in the first place. That man is not self-aware of his reality, and that man finds himself wanting more but not sure how to get it.

When we lose our identity, we forget our birth name and who we really are. Maybe we start lying to ourselves, turning to porn, drinking too much, having affairs, and ultimately turning away from God. Is any of this hitting too close to home right now?

I once remember being at a social event with my wife when the standard questioning came my way, "What's your name?" and "What do you do?" I don't honestly remember even providing my name before my wife answered for me. At that moment, I was hurt. I was exhausted from trying to figuring out who I was and what I wanted to be without any direction. But I mostly wanted to run to the man that I wanted to become.

The problem is, I didn't know who he was at that point or how to find him.

Have you experienced this?

Waking Up from the Dream

When I think about identity, I can't help but think of the movie scene from *National Lampoon's Christmas Vacation* (1989), where Clark Griswold, played by Chevy Chase, is having difficulty sleeping and strolls down to the kitchen. In the scene, Clark finds himself dreaming and staring out of his back window.

Clark's Christmas wish revolved around gifting his family a new backyard swimming pool. The movie revolves around Clark's constant concern about affording the pool without his Christmas bonus check, which is yet to arrive. In the movie scene, Clark is daydreaming about the joy the pool would bring.

However, his idyllic vision takes an unexpected turn when Cousin Eddie makes a peculiar appearance in Clark's daydream, decked out in a wifebeater shirt, flippers, and a leopard print banana hammock, all while drinking a beer. The dream then shifts to a fantasy involving a lingerie saleswoman he encountered earlier in the movie, who tantalizingly strips out of her bathing suit on the diving board of the pool. The scene ends when Cousin Eddie's daughter, Ruby Sue, thinks Clark is Santa Claus and wakes him from his dream.

Have you ever caught yourself staring out one of your windows, hoping for something that isn't there? Or perhaps you're staring out the window, wondering why it feels like everyone else has what you want. Perhaps you buy into cultural influences and ads because it looks like the "cool" thing to do.

You constantly compare yourself to others who seem to have more. But it's a mistake to set personal expectations based on false narratives. You get into trouble when you compromise your values in the pursuit of external validation. When individuals focus on what they don't have, it leads to a sense of inadequacy, impacting their self-perception and identity.

Moses and Identity
Losing your identity is an age-old problem. Consider the Biblical character of Moses. Born a Hebrew during a time of oppression, his destiny was intricately woven into the fabric of a divine plan. Moses started his journey as a shepherd, tending to his flock on the quiet hillsides. Little did he know that a profound struggle with identity and purpose would soon mark his life.

Like many men in their journeys through life, Moses faced the challenge of reconciling his origins with his present reality. The call to leadership came unexpectedly, as a burning bush ignited with the voice of God. Despite being chosen, Moses grappled with self-doubt and questioned his worthiness for the task. He felt the weight of his identity as a Hebrew conflicting with the expectations placed upon him as a leader.

Just as men today navigate through the complexities of societal expectations, family responsibilities, and personal aspirations, Moses found himself at a crossroads. His role as a husband and father added layers to his identity, forcing him to balance the demands of family life with the divine calling echoing in his ears.

The struggle reached its pinnacle when Moses, feeling the weight of his inadequacies, hid his face from God. In that moment, he mirrored the vulnerability that men often experience when confronted with their true selves. The journey of self-discovery is challenging, filled with moments of introspection and questioning, much like Moses faced on the sacred grounds of his encounter with the Almighty.

Yet, a resilient spirit emerged from the depths of Moses' internal conflict. He embraced his calling, leading his people through the trials of the desert and eventually standing before the parted waters of the Red Sea. Moses' metamorphosis from a hesitant shepherd to a revered leader reflects the transformative power of accepting one's identity and purpose.

Can you relate to Moses' internal conflict?

Moses' story is a timeless reminder that the journey of self-discovery and acceptance is a shared human experience. The struggle to reconcile identity, responsibilities, and aspirations is a universal theme that transcends time and cultural boundaries. As men, we navigate the intricate complexities of our lives, hoping to find inspiration like Moses' odyssey and the eventual triumph of embracing one's true calling.

Moses found what Clark Griswold was looking for: an identity isn't tied to a backyard pool, a luxury automobile, or winning the lottery; it's tied to having our identity in Christ. That's the good news; now, let's confront the first crucial aspect of our journey to self-discovery on our trip to finding more in life.

Lack of Self-Awareness and Identity Crisis

In the hustle of everyday life, it's not uncommon to feel adrift and uncertain about who you truly are. The absence of self-awareness creates a void in which an identity crisis festers. It's like navigating the sea without a compass, your ship tossed around by the waves of external expectations and societal pressures.

Why It Matters

Imagine going on a road trip without a map, a GPS, and or an overall plan to get where you want to go. Your spirit or internal compass guides every decision and action of your life's journey. Without a clear understanding of who you are, you risk constructing a life that doesn't resonate with your authentic self. This lack of alignment can lead to perpetual dissatisfaction, a sense of emptiness that echoes throughout your existence.

Like Moses, I experienced a phase in my life where I became disconnected from my current reality. While I didn't receive any revelations from a burning bush, the intensity of my struggles felt like I was engulfed in flames, and at times, that sensation lingers. I often defined my identity by being a CEO and perfectionist, projecting an image of having everything together. My self-perception was intertwined with images of a big house, a luxurious car, the latest golf equipment, and the latest styles of clothes.

Externally, I battled to maintain this façade, but internally, I struggled to survive. A persistent voice echoed in my mind, discouraging me with phrases like "You can't do it," "You're not worthy," and "That's impossible." It resembled the gloomy demeanor of Eeyore from Winnie-the-Pooh, lamenting, "It's the only cloud in the sky, and it's drizzling right on me. Somehow, I'm not surprised."

Truthfully, I wasn't self-aware enough to understand what was happening. I was in denial. I wouldn't accept any responsibility for solving my situation.

The Journey to Self-Awareness

I've come to realize that the key to forging an authentic identity begins with addressing one's lack of self-awareness. It involves stripping away the layers of societal conditioning and external influences to unveil the core of one's true self. Understanding oneself allows one to navigate life purposefully, steering clear of the tumultuous waters of an identity crisis.

Imagine, for a moment, standing at the crossroads of your thoughts, with each path leading to a part of your identity waiting to be discovered. The journey commences with introspection — a deliberate exploration of your values, beliefs, and aspirations. Take a moment to sit with your thoughts, unraveling the threads of influence woven into the fabric of your identity.

What do you see when you sit with your thoughts?

Now that we're back on the road let's talk about the power of introspection. Introspection isn't a mere glance in the mirror; it's a deep dive into the recesses of your mind. It's about asking yourself tough questions, confronting insecurities, and embracing your strengths. As you navigate this internal landscape, you'll uncover the nuances that make you unique through the power of introspection and self-examination. This is your opportunity to look in the mirror and take an honest assessment.

Why Self-Awareness is Important

Introspection is the compass that guides you through the vast terrain of your identity. It's not about judging yourself but understanding yourself — the quirks, the passions, the fears. This knowledge becomes the cornerstone of your authenticity, enabling you to make choices aligned with your true self.

Think of introspection as holding up a mirror to your soul. You can see your experiences, emotions, and aspirations in your reflection. It's about recognizing the patterns in your thoughts, understanding why certain things trigger joy or discomfort, and acknowledging the narratives that shape your perception.

This reflection matters because it bridges the gap between your conscious and subconscious mind. It unveils the layers of your identity that the noise of external influences may have obscured. This clarity empowers you to consciously shape your identity rather than being a passive recipient of societal expectations.

You may say, "Wow," that is a lot to take in. It's understandable if you find the concept of introspection overwhelming — it's indeed a substantial concept to absorb. I've personally struggled with the power that the subconscious mind has over our past events and traumas. These thoughts sit in the back of our minds and keep us hostage, stuck in a virtual prison.

The Quest for Self-Awareness

Here is an important point from a so-called "recovering perfectionist:" Embrace imperfections!

In the quest for self-awareness, perfection is not the goal. Embrace the imperfections, the scars, and the untidy corners of your identity. They tell a story of growth, resilience, and the beautiful messiness that makes you human.

This book is a great example of embracing imperfection. There was a time when accepting my vulnerabilities wasn't much of an option. Not so many years ago, I would have never attempted to write a book or host a podcast. You certainly would have never heard me talk about my story and express what I feel like I do on the True Man Podcast. You may be asking, what shifted?

Getting involved in a small men's group was a major shift. We didn't focus on who won Saturday's game or our favorite restaurant. Those things came up, but we focused more on our feelings, goals, families, and careers. We talked about how there was an alternative to flipping someone off in traffic and how to deal with our anger.

When you surround yourself with supportive individuals who encourage growth, you create an environment conducive to discovering your authenticity and vulnerability. Acknowledging imperfections allows a man to be vulnerable and open about his shortcomings. This authenticity fosters genuine connections with others, as we are often drawn to real and relatable people.

If you are willing to work with yourself and embrace imperfection, you'll be on your way to leading an authentic masculine life.

What are some ways you can do that?

First, recognize that you will make mistakes. Fear of showing imperfections may lead to strained relationships and cause you to create a fake-it-till-you-make-it mentality. Embracing your shortcomings means accepting that your faults and failures are a natural part of life. Once you accept your limitations, you can lead a more authentic life.

Remember that those mistakes are opportunities to learn and grow. This mindset encourages continuous learning and personal growth, as men can use setbacks as opportunities for improvement rather than viewing them as threats to their masculinity.

If you accept and showcase your flaws, others will see the real you. It's easier to relate to someone who is confidently showing their real self. This fosters deeper connections and allows men to express their true thoughts and emotions without fear of judgment.

When you do this, you position yourself to create healthier relationships. Acknowledging your mistakes allows you to communicate openly and honestly, creating a foundation of trust. The openness and transparency you begin to display will develop into the bedrock of trust people come to know and appreciate about you.

Does that reduce societal expectations and the unrealistic standards of perfection that some men feel? Does it reduce for you?

I have personally struggled with this, and I believe many other men do as well. There is a lot of pressure on men to behave, look, or feel a certain way to show their masculinity. Take, for example, physical appearance. Being short, overweight, or non-athletic doesn't make you any less of a man than someone who is tall, muscular, or has a chiseled jawline. Yet, the phrase tall, dark, and handsome has stood the test of time for what we should measure up to.

Another example is traditional gender norms that discourage men from expressing vulnerability or emotions other than anger. There is often an expectation for men to be stoic, tough, and unemotional, which can contribute to mental health challenges and hinder genuine emotional connections.

Embracing your imperfections liberates a man from the pressure to conform or measure up to societal "standards." What we are really talking about is having compassion for yourself. Instead of being overly critical or judgmental about yourself or others, it's far more important to develop a more understanding and forgiving attitude toward yourself. This will lead to improved mental well-being.

When you embrace the fact you won't win every game, win every business proposal, or hit every green light when you're driving, you open yourself up to enjoy life's little moments. Yes, it means you may fail, but at least you tried. You gave it a shot, and it didn't go how you wanted it to, but it opens you up to the question, *what will I do differently next time*?

Being genuine and sincere in our interactions with others, without putting on a façade or conforming to societal expectations or stereotypes of masculinity, allows us to express our emotions, desires, and vulnerabilities openly, without fear of judgment or rejection. It also means being comfortable with who we are and embracing our unique identity, regardless of societal pressures to conform to a certain mold of masculinity. Ultimately, being true to yourself allows you to live in alignment with your core values and beliefs.

Essentially, living in alignment with our core values and beliefs allows us to experience a more purposeful, authentic, and satisfying life. It's an ongoing process of self-reflection, self-discovery, and intentional decision-making, which we will discuss throughout this book.

Why Does the Journey Through Self-Awareness Matter?

I wanted to write this book so that I could share the introspection and life lessons I've learned with other men. I've realized that many men don't slow down long enough to gain the self-awareness that is necessary to live the fulfilling life they want.

You may live a happy life, but if you could really be filled with all the joys of the kingdom, would you slow down long enough to make it happen?

When I examined my life, I found perfection is an illusion that often leads to self-criticism and a relentless pursuit of an unattainable standard. Admitting my own imperfections was an act of self-compassion. It allowed me to appreciate my journey and my uniqueness and gain a sense of authenticity I didn't know existed.

My spiritual journey allowed me to understand that my life was more about trusting God and less about trusting me. Going through life "white knuckling," the steering wheel can lead to much dissatisfaction.

Have you experienced that kind of dissatisfaction?

Biblical View of Self-Awareness
The King James Version of the Bible does not explicitly use the term "introspection," nor does it use the term self-awareness. These concepts are more rooted in psychology and self-reflection. However, the Bible does contain verses that encourage self-examination, reflection, and seeking understanding. One notable verse is from the New Testament:

"Examine yourselves, whether ye be in the faith; prove your own selves. Know ye, not your own selves, how that Jesus Christ is in you, except ye be reprobates?"
2 Corinthians 13:5 (KJV)

Let's talk about the Apostle Paul and self-awareness to gain some perspective. In scripture, Paul's desire was not to resort to church discipline in Corinth; instead, he hoped for repentance among the wrongdoers. However, those engaged in immoral behavior were challenging Paul's apostolic authority. Paul intended to correct those who ignored his warnings and refused to repent before his imminent arrival (2 Corinthians 13:2–3). In response to their challenge, he urged them to introspect and assess their own faith.

This wasn't the first instance of Paul advising the Corinthians to practice self-examination. Earlier, he had observed the church participating in the Lord's Supper in an unworthy manner and urged them, *"Each person should examine themselves before they eat of the bread and drink from the cup" (1 Corinthians 11:28)*. Believers were encouraged to scrutinize their motives, actions, and the state of their hearts to avoid bringing God's discipline upon themselves.

Paul's primary concern was fostering spiritual health and wholeness within the Corinthian Christian community. If individuals were genuinely in the faith, they would recognize the indwelling presence of Jesus Christ within them. The Holy Spirit would be actively working, promoting sanctification and moral living.

Conversely, if their lives lacked evidence of the Spirit's activity, it indicated Christ was not dwelling within them, leading to a failure in the test.

This verse encourages believers to examine themselves, evaluate their faith, and recognize the presence of Jesus Christ within them. While the language may not directly refer to introspection, the underlying message aligns with self-reflection and examination.

What can we learn from the apostle Paul on our journey of life self-awareness? In modern terms, "check yourself at the door!" Before you yell, act, or throw something that will leave a gaping hole in the wall, stop! Examine yourself, pause, take a knee, and breathe!

In 1 Corinthians 11:28, the apostle Paul urged each person to "*examine themselves before they eat of the bread and drink from the cup;*" to remember Christ. If it's important enough to examine yourself before facing God, isn't it equally important to do it before you do something stupid?

If you examined yourself in the heat of the moment, how could you dramatically change the outcome of a situation?

Summary of Lack of Self-Awareness and Identity Crisis

A man's identity is crucial for living a fulfilled life. It's what defines him, sets him apart, and gives him purpose. Without a clear sense of who he is, a man can feel lost, directionless, and unfulfilled.

Knowing his identity means knowing his strengths, weaknesses, values, and beliefs. It's about understanding what he stands for and wants to achieve. A man with a strong sense of identity can make decisions confidently, pursue his goals passionately, and navigate challenges with resilience.

Identity shapes a man's relationships, too. It influences how he interacts with others, forms connections, and contributes to his community. A man who knows himself well can build meaningful relationships based on honesty, respect, and authenticity.

Furthermore, a man's identity gives him a sense of belonging and pride. Whether it's his cultural background, profession, or personal achievements, his identity gives him a place in the world and a sense of accomplishment.

Ultimately, a man's identity is the foundation of his happiness and fulfillment. It gives him the confidence to embrace who he is, pursue his dreams, and live life on his own terms. Without it, he may struggle to find purpose and satisfaction in his journey. So, embracing and understanding his identity is essential for any man who wants to live a truly fulfilling life.

Scan the code above with your smartphone
to view my chapter wrap-up video.

Go to this link to access the Chapter Worksheets:
https://truemanlifecoaching.com/TrueManTrueWaysWorksheets

Rest Stop

In the following pages, journal and reflect on your thoughts about being more self-aware of your true identity.

_____

_____

_____

_____

_____

_____

_____

_____

_____

_____

_____

_____

_____

_____

_____

_____

_____

_____

_____

_____

_____

_____

TRUE MAN

Chapter Two

Journaling Your Journey

True Man Tip

A word of caution before we begin this chapter.
Do not journal while driving,
but certainly journal everywhere else.
Thank you!
Now you may proceed.

Writing for me has become an outlet. I find myself amazed at what happens when I take the time to stop and put my thoughts down on paper. This book is a great example. Writing a book isn't easy. It is the culmination of the ideas and reflections that have been germinating in my head for some time. Some of those thoughts go out on the True Man Podcast, others in blogs, perhaps on social media, and some are never to be seen. Lucky you, I've only included the best of the best in this book.

I want to get you thinking about the importance of the journalling practice and incorporating it into your life. At the end of each chapter, I've included journaling areas with thought-provoking questions to get you started.

Now, more than ever, it's critical to practice continuous self-care to balance mental, physical, and spiritual health. One way to achieve this is by recording your thoughts and experiences through the age-old act of journaling. This is the True Man's way of giving yourself the time to reflect on your life and to process everything you've been through.

The earliest known writing was invented in ancient Mesopotamia around 3400 B.C. Local materials influenced the development of a Sumerian script: clay for tablets and reeds for styluses.[1] In Biblical times, plant fibers and animal skins were the primary writing surfaces utilized by scribes to write scripture. Early parchment was made of leather and is said to have been invented in the 2nd Century B.C. in Turkey.[2] The oldest known papyrus (plant) fragment dates back to 2900 B.C.[3]

Throughout history, people have been jotting down thoughts and details. Early diaries and journals were frequently kept as public records.[4] These remarkable documents have shifted from public works to private life recordings.

We've been recording our thoughts in pictures and writing since the beginning of time.

The written word is undoubtedly one of humanity's most potent and impactful creations ever devised. Writing enables the sharing of ideas, memories, experiences, and stories, as well as other parts of the human experience, in a way that nothing else does. Writing enables us to recognize and comprehend our

---

[1] Brown, Shelby. "Where Did Writing Come From?" Getty News. Getty Museum, April 27, 2021. https://www.getty.edu/news/where-did-writing-come-from/.

[2] "Parchment." In *Encyclopedia Britannica*. Accessed August 8, 2024. https://www.britannica.com/topic/parchment.

[3] Capua, Rebecca. "Papyrus-Making in Egypt: Essay: The Metropolitan Museum of Art: Heilbrunn Timeline of Art History." Papyrus-Making in Egypt, March 2015. https://www.metmuseum.org/toah/hd/pyma/hd_pyma.htm.

[4] Badgesforall. "The History of Journaling and Famous Journals." Web log. *Badges for All* (blog). Badges for All, January 8, 2020. https://badgesforall.wordpress.com/2020/01/08/the-history-of-journaling-and-famous-journals/.

history and past by assisting in the documentation of people, places, and events. It allows the exchange of intellectual ideas and concepts that have helped to shape cultures, governments, ideologies, sciences, and technologies.

Perhaps more crucially, the written word binds us together in ways no other medium can. By recording our ideas, tales, and recollections openly, we create an enduring record of ourselves and our lives. The written word transcends time and distance. When we read the words recorded by someone in the distant past or in a distant location, we are instantly transported into their mind and thoughts, connecting us closely to their life, ideas, and experiences.

How do you currently record your thoughts?

I share this background and history because it provides great insight into the potential power of recording our thoughts by journaling. Whether your thoughts are done in anger, for business, pleasure, creativity, or inspiration, the power of getting thoughts down on paper is endless.

I believe that the Holy Spirit uses journaling as a powerful tool to help us become more Christlike. This is a crucial part of your journey to become a True Man.

Writing or creating art in whatever form allows us to pause and attend to our inner being. Words may come readily or take a long time to produce. In either case, writing enables us to reflect on, contemplate, and thoroughly digest life's occurrences. Proverbs 4 emphasizes the critical nature of knowledge acquisition at all costs. Its phrases encourage deliberateness and vigilance:

"My son, pay close attention to everything I say; listen to my words. Keep them in your eyes and in your heart; they are vital to people who discover them and to the complete

body's wellness. Preserve your heart above all else, as it is the source of all your accomplishments. Allow your eyes to travel straight forward; keep a focused gaze directly ahead of you. Take caution when choosing your pathways and persevere in all your pursuits. Avoid wickedness with your foot."

(Proverbs 4:20–26)

Journaling can help us pay attention and redirect our thoughts toward information. Additionally, it can act as a safeguard for our hearts while we search for our inner selves, paying attention to what is happening in our hearts and submitting it to God.

While the biblical Psalms are not real "journaling," they reveal how our experiences can coexist with the truth of who God is. The broad themes and unashamed candor of the Psalms demonstrate how we can be entirely honest with ourselves and God about our feelings and ideas. Through journaling, we can communicate with God and be reminded of His majesty. Mary cherishes and considers the events surrounding Jesus' birth, according to Luke 2:19. *"The handiwork of the LORD is marvelous."* In Psalm 111:2, David reminds us to reflect on God's creation. *"The works of the Lord are great, sought out of all them that have pleasure therein."* Journaling can help us contemplate God's goodness and express our thankfulness to Him.

Additionally, journaling provides a written record for future reference. In times of spiritual desolation or despair, you can consult your journal to take encouragement from God's past faithfulness or reminders of truth. God regularly directed the Israelites to erect memorials. In Exodus 12, we learn that the Passover was created to serve as a reminder of God's faithfulness in rescuing the Israelites from Egypt. God commanded Joshua to raise monument stones following the Israelites' dry land passage of the Jordan River *"to act as a marker in your midst. When your children ask, 'What do these stones mean?' explain that the Jor-*

dan's flow was halted prior to the ark of the Lord's covenant. When it crossed the Jordan, it rendered the Jordan's waters inaccessible. These stones will forever serve as a reminder to the Israeli people." (Joshua 4: 6-8).

Psalms 77 and 143 emphasize the importance of remembering God's deeds through difficult times. Journals can be an effective tool for recalling God's activities throughout our own histories.

Journaling allows "natural" writers to actively use their gifts to mature in Christ. They can journal on biblical truths, or the lessons God may teach them via their current circumstances. Through your writing, you can reflect on the past and learn from your mistakes. You can also pray with God to reveal hidden truths along the road, or to assist in healing. Additionally, we might use journals to communicate our future aspirations and ambitions to God.

Journaling may be exciting to some while being tedious to others. Journaling does not come in a one-size-fits-all package and its impact can vary greatly from person to person. While journaling is not necessary for Christian growth, it can be a very beneficial tool for overall growth.

Beginning Your Journaling Journey

At this point, you may ask how to begin your journaling experience. Let's take a look.

Beginning your journaling isn't something that you need to think about too hard. Yes, there are numerous types and styles of journals and ways to do this, but the most important part is to begin by taking action and starting. Simply get some paper (or your computer) and start today.

- **Dust Off Your Pen and Paper** – You don't need anything special to keep a journal. Purists believe using pen and paper is the best way to journal because you can carry it anywhere, and you don't need technology. So, there are no excuses.

- **Do It First Thing in the Morning** – Don't procrastinate about keeping your journal. It may be best to do it in the morning before you begin your day so that you have the right frame of mind for the day. Plus, you only need five to ten minutes, so it's not that big of a deal.
- **Do It Last Thing at Night** – Another time to do it is before bed. This works especially well for gratitude journals. That way, you can go to sleep thinking about all the things you are grateful for instead of what you're worried about.
- **Write Every Single Day** – Whenever you choose to do it, try to set it up so that it becomes a ritual and a habit. Journaling every single day is going to be more effective than just doing it when you feel like it.
- **Start Simple** – Don't worry about style and substance right now; just work on the daily habit with pen and paper (or, if it's easier for you, a computer or smartphone). Don't make it hard - just get going.
- **Begin Today** – Start right now and write about your day. That's the easiest thing to do. Did anything significant happen today? How did you feel about it? What would you do differently? Would you make the same choices?
- **Try Different Types of Journals** – Once you develop the habit, you can start trying different types of journaling, like a bullet journal, a vision journal, or maybe even a project journal for your next project. (More on these different styles of journal is included later in this chapter.)
- **Keep It Private** – The main thing to remember about your journal is that it should be kept private. The only exception is if you want to share thoughts with a therapist, counselor, or coach or if you want to turn it into a book or course to help someone else overcome the same problem as you did.

Keeping a journal will help you deal with your life. The main reason is that writing it down helps you remember what you did right and what you did wrong. It helps you improve your decision-making capacity for similar situations. The main thing is to get started journaling in any way that works for you.

Achieve True Man Goals

Journaling can help you achieve your goals because it will force you to think about them, consider the why and how of them, and delve deeper into the situation so that you can examine all sides of it. Read on to find out how journaling can help.

- **It Forces You to Write Down Your Goals.** When you start a journal, it basically is a way to force yourself to document your goals. It doesn't matter whether you write them down on paper or you use technology to get it all down. Once they're written, they are ready to tackle.
- **It Makes You Consider the Why and How**. As you enter data into your journal, you'll be forced to face *why* you have these goals and *how* to achieve them. This is especially true if you write down a goal and focus on it in your journal.
- **It Enables You to Examine the Opportunities and Threats**. When you focus on goal-making with your journal, you'll be able to explore opportunities that may arise, as well as any obstacles in your path. This helps you avoid roadblocks in advance.
- **It Makes You Develop Steps for Success Based on Your Goals**. When you see it written down, you'll want to notice and pull out any steps you've developed in your journal and put them in your calendar for scheduling.
- **It Helps You Improve Goal Setting and Achievement**. Each time you intentionally set goals and define steps to achieve them, you are setting yourself up to improve your skills.

- **It Provides Accountability**. Even if no one else is reading your journal, a private journal can help you become accountable to yourself. If you develop the habit of looking at your journal and adding something else in there each day, it will help you take charge of your life and goals.
- **It Provides a Permanent Record.** Having a permanent record of the things you've done in your life, whether it's personal or work, is a beautiful thing. Hardly anyone has a perfect memory, so you'll maintain the lessons learned better with the record to look back at.
- **It May Be Inspirational**. Depending on the journal, you might even be able to take the information inside and compile it into a real book for others to read to inspire them. You might also take steps for your success in a project and turn it into a course to inspire someone else.

Journaling can help you set better goals because the process of entering facts in your journal will make you see them in a more logical and useful way. It is an excellent way to work toward accomplishing your vision of the future.

Creating Better Mental Health

Keeping any type of journal will help with improving mental health issues. However, if you really want to tackle a specific problem you're having, it will help to determine the right type of journal to keep. Keeping a particular kind of journal may work best for your issue.

- **Boosts Your Mood** – If you really want to boost your mood, keeping a gratitude journal is where it's at. All you need to do is write down what you're grateful for that day, once a day, before bed. It might not seem like much, but it's very powerful for going to sleep while thinking positively about your life.
- **Increases Your Sense of Well-Being** – As you write out your thoughts, you'll start seeing issues from a new angle

because you're opening your mind to think about them differently. This is going to make you feel more capable of dealing with whatever happens.

- **Reduces Anxiety** – The problem with anxiety is that it is designed to help us get away from immediate danger. It triggers the "fight or flight" response. If each time you have that anxious feeling, you choose to write in your journal about how you are feeling and why, you'll start to control it better.
- **Lowers Avoidance Behaviors** – Many people who have mental health issues practice avoidance behaviors like turning down new job opportunities or avoiding relation-ships and social events that make them feel anxious. When you write it out, it helps you get the feelings out real-istically, so you won't avoid it but will be OK with doing it.
- **You'll Sleep Better** – Pouring your heart out into a journal is a great way to get things off your chest. However, if you need a good night's rest, write in your gratitude journal right before bed. This way, you can go to sleep thinking of everything you have to be grateful for.
- **Makes You a Kinder Person** – Exploring your own emo-tional state and accepting your own feelings while you work through what makes you who you are in your jour-nal will make you naturally more empathetic to others. Letting go of judgment about yourself also improves your thoughts for others.
- **Improves Your Memory** – This is almost a situation where you want to say "duh," but it has to be said. Writing down things helps you remember them not only because you can go back and read them but also because the act of writing something down enables you to recall it.

One thing that helps you make your journaling work is learning how to keep one effectively. Make some journaling rules, do it every day to create a habit, and keep it private unless you decide to let your therapist see it or use it to help others. This is for you and only you.

Combating Loneliness with Journals

It really doesn't matter what your issue is; if you want to overcome it, you can find a way to use journaling to help. You can set up a particular type of journal, like a gratitude journal, to help yourself become more thankful for what you do have. You can also keep a bullet journal and set goals to overcome the loneliness that many men experience. The possibilities are truly endless.

Let's look in more detail at how journaling can help combat loneliness. It can allow you to explore your thoughts and emotions surrounding the loneliness that you are experiencing. If you can write about each part of your feelings and when you first noticed them, you may identify the core cause of the feelings. When you do that, you can develop a plan to solve the problem or challenge.

Let's Take a Look at Other Beneficial Aspects of Journaling:

Writing is a time-honored way of expressing thoughts and feelings safely. You never have to let anyone read it. You can write letters to friends, family members, yourself, or even to someone you don't know. You keep these for yourself when you're done to bring them out into the "light" to study and assess.

Journaling can provide a way to understand deeper parts of yourself. Sometimes, you may have difficulty articulating what you are feeling and why. After all, it can be hard to express our vulnerabilities, even to ourselves. But when you focus on writing it down, it can help you understand everything in a new way from a new direction that you may not have considered.

It might seem like a strange notion to consider, but writing can even help you foster social connections. As you read through your journal entries, you'll discover ways to overcome your situation to find the healthy social connections you need.

Journaling can help you see the big picture more easily. Looking back at the things you've written over time about any topic can provide insight into the situation that you never saw coming. That's because having a journal to look back on provides a way to see your problems in a different light. You may feel super-lonely today, but it's still less than yesterday, which lets you know it's going to get even better from here.

Journaling provides a means to understand and organize your thoughts. Writing things down, especially when you choose a particular method, like the bullet journal, will help you get your thoughts down in an organized and useful way. When your thoughts are a jumble, you might not see the real point, but when they're organized, it makes all the difference. For example, in writing it all down, you may realize that your loneliness is really due to being with the wrong people, people who do not value you.

Journaling can sharpen your observation skills. Once you start writing regularly and it's become a habit, something amazing will happen. Your observation skills will be sharper, and you'll have an easier time coming up with descriptive and expressive words to use in your journal. This is going to lead to more clarity in your observations and experiences.

Journaling can help create more gratitude in your life. Something funny happens when you commit to journaling every day. What happens is that as you're writing (even if you're upset), you'll become calmer - especially when you read it back. You'll become grateful for what you do have that is positive in your life, even if it's simply the ability to breathe in and out today.

If you want to combat loneliness, consider writing about and exploring why you feel lonely. You should also remember to read the definition of "loneliness" to ensure that this is what you are really experiencing. No one ever needs to be lonely, even when they are alone, if they know how to work through your thoughts and feelings. Journaling can help with that.

Journaling Can Help You Cope with Stress

Stress affects almost everyone at some time in their lives. Feeling stressed can come from a number of different factors in your life, such as your job, relationship issues, or even past events. Whatever the reason you are stressed, congratulations for recognizing it and wanting to do something about it.

Here are some good ways to journal to help combat your stress:

- **Write daily for 5 to 15 minutes.** The important thing about journaling is that you need to do it daily long term for it to really work. It takes a lot of writing and insight to figure out why you're dealing with stress and how to overcome it.
- **Write about your worries to gain clarification.** Go straight to the issues and describe them from every single angle you can come up with. The more descriptive you are, the better. Go back to the first time you felt this way about this topic so that you can get to the bottom of it.
- **Write about the present.** What's going on in the present for you? Put out of your mind what you did, what someone else did, or what can be done - write about precisely what is happening right now and where you stand with the issue causing your stress. If it's generalized stress, try to make a list of things that might be contributing.
- **Describe the worst thing but be realistic.** We often get stressed thinking about the unknown or the "worst thing" that could possibly happen. Instead of worrying about all the possibilities, describe this worst thing but make

it realistic. For example, a train falling out of the sky on your house isn't very likely. However, bad weather, rude neighbors, and or someone rejecting your idea is a more accurate outcome. Sometimes, looking at the worst thing that can happen brings peace.

- **On the flip side, document the best that can happen.** Think and write about the very best rational outcome of the situation you're anxious about. Include potential steps and tactics to achieve this best-case scenario so that you can see it to fruition if you choose.

- **Document what is really happening.** As you are writing, be very careful to be grounded and honest above all else. Other than when you imagine the best and worst, ensure that you are also documenting the reality of what is happening to you right now. That way, you can narrow down identifying the stress-inducing situation.

- **Write a counter-argument to yourself.** A really good way to overcome some stress about a situation is to argue with yourself. First, tell your story as a letter to yourself about what is happening. Then, write a letter back to yourself in answer, arguing against all the negativity and turning it into positivity. If your best friend had written that, what would you have said back?

Are you surprised that writing can accomplish so much? If you go into journaling with an open mind, a good attitude, and specific goals, you can achieve a lot. The important thing is that you need to be honest with yourself so that you can find out the true causes of your stress. In this way, the actions you take to overcome it really are effective.

Use a Gratitude Journal
It might seem like a pipe dream that writing in a journal could be so beneficial. But the scientific evidence is in, and gratitude does

benefit you in big ways[5] especially if you keep a gratitude journal for the long term and use it daily.

- **Experience stronger and more fulfilling relationships.** It's so simple, but it can be hard to accept that you are the one who makes yourself happy with your own choices. Another person cannot make you happy or grateful. Only you can do that. But something amazing happens when you express gratitude often – your relationships simply open up and become better. If they don't, you will start to recognize them for what they are and let them go.
- **Become physically healthier.** Being grateful for the ability to move and breathe will eventually cross over into wanting to ensure that you can always do that. Therefore, you'll be more motivated to go on walks, eat right, stay hydrated, and live in gratitude for every aspect of your life.
- **Increase your mental dexterity.** The ability to take "lemons and turn them into lemonade" can be gained by keeping a gratitude journal. This kind of journal shows that even a bad day has some good in it. That requires a good imagination, creativity, and thinking on your feet.
- **Feel less aggression in your life.** It's hard to be angry if you are happy and grateful. It's okay to be outraged about injustices in the world without being aggressive. But if you feel constantly frustrated, you may not be recognizing the many things for which you should be grateful. Most people can find something in their lives to be thankful for.
- **Become more empathetic.** As you write more, seeking to fill your mind with thoughts of gratitude, you will start seeing others differently. You'll have more ability to put yourself in their shoes and see things their way without judgment. It happens when you learn to forgive yourself.

---

[5] Courtney E. Ackerman, MA. "Benefits of Gratitude: 28+ Surprising Research Findings." PositivePsychology.com, June 26, 2024. https://positivepsychology.com/benefits-gratitude-research-questions/.

- **Get more restful sleep.** If you go to sleep each night feeling thankful for everything you've experienced (or at least most of it), you'll find you have less anxiety, and it will be easier to sleep.
- **Get more done every day.** Due to feeling more rested, less stressed, and more grateful, you'll have a lot more energy to get things done every day. That's always going to make you feel even more thankful because good things can happen due to productivity.
- **Feel better about yourself.** You can't help but feel better about yourself when you have improved so many good qualities about yourself. Your self-esteem will go up when you express gratitude for what your mind and body can do for you.

If you want to be happier, get more done, and experience real joy in your life, a gratitude journal can be the way to achieve it. Remember and accept that you are in control. Accepting that you do have control is half the battle, and your journal will help you realize this important fact.

Different Types of Journals

When you begin journaling, it will likely occur to you that having more than one type of journal might be the best way to keep everything organized. When you have more than one type of journal, you can simply go to the specific journal to work on one issue at a time or keep something organized so you can make better decisions.

1. **Bullet Journals** – This type of journal is useful for anyone who has lots of to-do lists, loves using a pen and paper, and enjoys goal tracking. Your journal should have a table of contents that you create as you add to the journal so you can find things. You'll use symbols, colors, and lines to make your bullet journal. You should be able to understand what's on the page at a glance.

2. **Vision Journals** – You may have heard of vision boards, and this is essentially it, except it's a journal that helps lead you to your vision. The way it works is that you set up the journal to have only one goal per page. Then, you can write words, add pictures, or draw something that enables you to make plans to reach that goal. When you do reach the goal, be sure to go back and add the date of achievement.

3. **Line a Day Journals** – Basically, this journal is what it's called – you write down only one line a day. You will simply write a short summary about what you did that day. It should be only a sentence or two and should not take up that much space in your journal. Some people like using a calendar and a pen for this.

4. **Classic Journal** – This is simply a diary, and you can write whatever you want in it every day. It can be long or short, and you can skip days if you want. The classic journal is just like the diary that you may have kept as a child.

5. **Prayer Journal** – This is a particular type of journal where you essentially act like your diary or journal is your higher power. Write your prayers to God instead of saying them. Write them down so you remember them and can look back and reflect on them.

6. **Dream Journal** – Some people really like tracking their dreams because they believe that dreams provide signs for life. To keep a dream journal, you have to train yourself to record what happened in your dream every morning while it is still fresh in your mind. Write about the dream and then research what it means, and write about that, too.

7. **Food Journal** – Write down everything you eat every day. Some people like to include calories, carbohydrates, fat content, etc. It can also help to write down why you ate it, when you ate it, how you felt about eating it, etc.

8. **Travel Journal** – A wonderful way to remember your travels is to keep a travel journal. Some people like making one for each trip so that it's easier to remember. You can write your thoughts in your journal and attach tickets, pics, and memories.
9. **Gratitude Journal** – We discussed the benefits of keeping a gratitude journal above. Remember, nothing can be negative in this journal because it's designed to help you think more positively.
10. **Project Journal** – This is a handy journal to keep, especially for anyone who regularly works on projects. Keeping a journal of each project you undertake allows you to see the actions, decisions, plans, results, and data concerning that project. That data will help you improve every project but will also help you look back on this one with excitement.

If you need to work through a specific problem, keeping journals for different things is an effective approach. Journaling is also a great way to organize and use your thoughts and memories for the future.

Journaling in Your Daily Routine

The best way to see the benefits of journaling is to stick with it for the long term. Long-term journaling allows you to look to the past and present to find new perspectives and insights about your life. But first, you have to do it. And you need to do it daily to make it a habit. Let's review a few tips for making journaling part of your daily routine.

- **Make It Easy** – Don't make it a huge deal, and it'll be simpler to get done. For example, many people find using a notebook and paper more accessible than a computer. You can have the book in your bag, on your bedside table, or wherever you plan to write in it.

- **Choose a Time That Works** – The best times to do it are early morning, first thing, or the last thing before you go to bed. However, that might not work for some people. Find a time that will work for you. For example, some people like journaling during lunch, at their desk in the study, or in a park, or sitting outside on their deck. It's up to you.
- **Get a Drink and Eat a Snack** – You don't want to have any excuses or extraneous thoughts while you're writing in your journal. Make sure you're fed and hydrated.
- **Create a Comfortable and Accessible Space** – It's easier to get into your thoughts if you're comfortable and not thinking about how bad your tailbone or wrist hurts. Some people like using a desk, a comfy couch, or an easy chair to write, others prefer to write in bed.
- **Combine It with Something Else You Enjoy Doing** – If you enjoy cleaning the house with the windows open and the breeze flowing in, why not journal at that moment? If it's a daily thing, take a break and add journaling to it, and it will create a habit fast.
- **Add Some Relaxing Music to Set the Mood** – Now, it's true that some people prefer silence, so that's fine if you do. But try relaxing music that doesn't have words to help you gather your thoughts and stay calm and focused.
- **Use Your Favorite Type of Journal** – For some people, using a specific (like bullet or prayer journaling) works better since those formats give some helpful parameters for beginners.
- **Consider Using Journaling Prompts** – Writer's block happens to everyone, but prompts can help you figure out what to write when you feel stuck. You can find many different types of journaling prompts online. For example,

Calm has a list of 12 Gratitude Journal Prompts[6], or you can check out 64 Journal Prompts for Self-Discovery.[7]

- **Reward Yourself** – When you have been diligent for a month writing in your journal, take some time to read what you wrote - then reward yourself for doing it. You might buy some colored pens or scrapbooking materials to add some definition and interest to your journal.

To truly experience the full benefits of journaling, you must find a way to incorporate it into your everyday life. The best way to accomplish this is to make it easy and turn it into a habit.

You can talk about positives and negatives, the pros and cons of decisions made that day, or talk about something that thrilled or excited you. Keeping a journal can assist you in bringing some order to your chaotic world. You can better understand yourself by exploring your most private thoughts, feelings, and emotions.

Consider journaling as your time to unwind, release some stress, and recenter yourself. Locate a peaceful space to write and acknowledge that your journaling practice benefits both your mind and body. By reminding yourself that you are the author of your life's story, you can journal your way into a new chapter of your life and begin your walk as a True Man.

---

[6] "12 Gratitude Journal Prompts to Add to Your Self-Care Routine." Web log. *Calm* (blog). Calm. Accessed August 8, 2024. https://www.calm.com/blog/gratitude-journal-prompts.

[7] Raypole, Crystal. "Ready, Set, Journal! 64 Journaling Prompts for Self-Discovery." Psych Central, May 17, 2021. https://psychcentral.com/blog/ready-set-journal-64-journaling-prompts-for-self-discovery.

Scan the code above with your smartphone
to view my chapter wrap-up video.

Go to this link to access the Chapter Worksheets:
https://truemanlifecoaching.com/TrueManTrueWaysWorksheets

Rest Stop

**In the following pages, journal and reflect on
your thoughts about journaling your journey.**

_____

_____

_____

_____

_____

_____

_____

_____

_____

_____

_____

_____

_____

_____

_____

_____

_____

_____

_____

_____

_____

_____

MIKE VAN PELT

Chapter Three

True Man and the Open Road

True Man Tip

You define what a True Man is.
But choose wisely.
It is your legacy.

What is a True Man?
Why Would You Want to Become One?

I believe this book helps define the attributes of a True Man, but the reality is I could have included so much more. However, what I've come to discover is that only you can define what a True Man is for you. Only you can set up your road map; you set the perimeters of your road trip through life; only you can go on the open road journey. However, you define it, living the life of a True Man can be a beautiful place to be in.

I love the idea of being a True Man, especially at this midpoint in my life. It just sounds like a refreshing way to live, like standing next to the ocean on a hot summer day with the waves crashing around me. Or, how about a sunny day in the mountains with a light breeze to cool you off? Any way you slice it, becoming a True Man feels so good.

The journey of life has gotten me to this point. I think more about my legacy and less about what might have been versus what can be. I've forgiven myself for the stupid things I've done and the people I've hurt. Road rage seems to make a lot less sense. Seeing how many cans of beer I can drink and how late I can stay up are things of the past.

I don't want to be angry, sad, lonely, or mystified by wondering if the world is conspiring against me. These things don't feel good, and I no longer like camping out in them. Why one would do it in the first place is certainly a matter of choice, and I often chose wrong.

Is my story unique, or am I a special case? Not by long a shot, more men than not have traveled the same path I did. Some learn faster than others, and some men never learn at all. I think many men hit this crossroads in their lives at a certain point, and things can crash around them if they are not prepared. I'm not sure how you prevent the crash without the journey, but perhaps we can be better prepared for the next "it" when it happens, and it will happen. Maybe we can do it with a lot less damage by making it easier and faster to recover.

I know this: a man can't be true without being oriented in God's word and having a few good teammates, wingmen, accountability partners, or good buddies to get through life's daily challenges.

And thus, the founding of *True Man*.

The True Man Beginning

True Man began, like all innocent things do, with a hope and a dream. My friend Paul Baily and I wanted to make a small difference in the world by bringing men together in a small group. We were just two guys who felt the idea of business networking had gone from giving to taking, and we set out to change that.

Rather quickly, we realized that forming a faith-based group was what we wanted. In our small group, we could have thoughtful conversations and build relationships that were more than an inch deep. Our experiences taught us that many men were missing out on opportunities to look inside themselves under the mentorship of others. Through our framework, men could form the deeper and more profound Christian friendships that they so desperately longed for.

The inspiration for this book stems from the development of our men's small group that met at Paul's office on a weekly basis. As I spoke about at the beginning of the book, it also stems from hitting the road to one of our favorite coffee shops, Open Road Roastery, in Columbus, North Carolina.

There is something to be said about being in a car and experiencing the "open road" with a friend. Road trips provide an opportunity to bond and talk. It's the shared adventure of navigating unfamiliar roads or enjoying scenic views. It's about time away and pausing from the routine of life. It's about escaping the stress we find ourselves under and putting the pressures of the day behind us.

In many respects, the open road is a metaphor for a man's life and the journey or path that we go on. The road of life captures a dynamic and evolving adventure with various twists, turns, and unknown destinations.

Each man embarks on his own journey, navigating the open road with a sense of anticipation and curiosity. The road is lined with milestones representing achievements, crossroads symbolizing choices, and scenic overlooks offering moments of reflection.

As he travels, the road presents challenges – steep hills to climb, unexpected detours, and occasional rough patches. Yet, these challenges are not obstacles but rather opportunities for growth and resilience. The vehicle he drives is his character, powered by determination and fueled by the experiences gathered along the way.

The open road is not a solitary path but a shared adventure. Traveling with a friend like Paul not only made the trip more fun, it also allowed us to share stories and insights, and it gave us opportunities to grow and learn from each other. Relationships are the rest stops, where connections are forged, and the shared laughter and tears become cherished memories.

True Man Obstacles

During those road trips, lunches, and phone calls, Paul and I theorized what was going on with men around the globe. From our standpoint, masculinity was in trouble. Wounded hearts and brokenness seemed like the norm rather than the fulfilling life we believed men should be leading. All around us, we saw divorce and suicide rates skyrocketing. Men are lonelier and more unchurched than ever before, and this has left them scrambling to find a purpose in life.

You could call our perspective a hypothesis of sorts, but unfortunately, our analysis wasn't wrong. According to a survey completed by the Survey Center on American Life and conducted in May 2021, 15% of men in America have no close friends. In 1990, only 3% of men reported having no close friends; by 2021, the number had risen to 15%. More than one in four (28%) men under the age of 30 reported having no close social connections.[8]

While rates of loneliness have subsided from a high of 25% in 2021 to 17% in 2023[9] 15% of men still report that they have no close friends.[10] As if that's not enough, a 35-year study by

---

[8]   Cox, Daniel A. "The State of American Friendship: Change, Challenges, and Loss." American Survey Center, June 8, 2021. https://www.americansurveycenter.org/research/ the-state-of-american-friendship-change-challenges-and-loss/.

[9]   Witters, Dan. "Loneliness in U.S. Subsides from Pandemic High." Gallup. com, February 7, 2024. https://news.gallup.com/poll/473057/loneliness-subsides-pandemic-high.aspx.

[10] Cox, The State of American Friendship

Brigham Young University, using data from 3.4 million people, found that individuals who suffered from loneliness or isolation, or even those who simply lived alone, saw their risk of premature death rise by up to 32%.

According to a US Surgeon General's report, lack of social connection is associated with a 29% increased risk of heart disease and a 32% increased risk of stroke. It is also associated with an increased risk for anxiety, depression, and dementia. One study found that, in terms of damage to your health, loneliness was the equivalent of smoking 15 cigarettes a day.[11]

As if those numbers aren't bad enough, the suicide rate for males is stunningly bad. According to the Movember Foundation, Men are 4 times more likely than women to take their own lives.[12] In Canada and the U.S., the highest suicide rates are among white men in their 50s (except for men over 75 in the U.S.).[13]

Sadly, we're not sure why.

There's rarely just one factor that explains a person's choice to end their life, and it's likely the same applies to suicide rates. Higher rates of drug and alcohol use, as well as employment and economic issues, may be factors in the higher rates of suicides in men, but the issue hasn't been studied enough to be sure.

---

[11] Office of the Surgeon General (OSG). Our Epidemic of Loneliness and Isolation: The U.S. Surgeon General's Advisory on the Healing Effects of Social Connection and Community. US Department of Health and Human Services, 2023.

[12] "Movember: Changing the Face of Men's Health! " Gatorcare." GatorCare, November 1, 2022. https://gatorcare.org/2022/11/01/movember-changing-the-face-of-mens-health/#:~:text=Men%20are%204%20times%20more.hesitate%20to%20ask%20for%20help.

[13] "Schwartz, Daniel. "Suicide Rates Are Highest for Men in Their 50s and We're Not Sure Why." https://www.cbc.ca/news/health/suicide-men-50s-causes-1.3263412 CBC News. November 6, 2015.

So, what are the reasons for so many suicides by men in their 50s, and why has that rate gone up faster than any other age group?

Now, here is an interesting quote from a scientific perspective, so read with caution.

What's striking is how little we really understand about why the numbers peak when men are in their 50s. Psychologist Dan Bilsker studies this issue, and he notes that the reasons behind the spike are complicated and concerning. "It doesn't fit previous models of things driving suicidal behavior." In those models, by their 50s, men should feel "more in control of their lives, have worked out a lot of issues, and be coping pretty well," he says. After all, most of them are working, and they've had jobs, relationships, children, and life experiences. So, the high suicide rate "raises a more disturbing model."[14]

Let me ask you, as a man, do you always feel in control of your life? Do you always have things worked out? Are all your relationships as good as they can be because you're in your 50s?

I am not a psychologist, but I can look at these problems from a Christian perspective. I believe that the devil has a hand in the increased suicides among men. But those outside of the Christian faith don't understand this philosophy, don't know how to seek help, or are unwilling to seek out the light. What's clear is that men are struggling to find answers when they need them, and they need the help of a few good men and a loving God to support them.

If you take the risk factors for suicide alone, we find that many of these factors are also part of the guilt, shame, and wounds that men walk around with every day and everywhere:

---

[14] https://pmc.ncbi.nlm.nih.gov/articles/PMC6109879/

- Divorce or relationship breakdowns
- Being bullied at school, college, or work
- History of physical and sexual abuse
- Inability to form or sustain meaningful relationships
- Using drugs and/or alcohol to help cope with emotions, relationships, the pressure of work, or other issues
- Social isolation or living alone
- Physical pain and illness, living alone, and feelings of hopelessness and guilt.

And the list goes on!

Although Paul and I didn't know these statistics at the time, it was clear to us (and later confirmed by the evidence) that men and their relationships were in crisis. It's easy to get overwhelmed by the numbers, but in reality, the best thing we could do was jump in and figure out how to manage our group and help the men in our lives.

True Man evolved from a group to a podcast, and it is now on a mission to help men achieve more as men, fathers, and spouses. As it turns out, doing life on your own or on your own terms is terribly difficult, if not impossible. It's important to have a group of open and honest men rooting for you as much as they are for their own success.

One of the reasons I created the "True Man Podcast" was to connect with men who share the search for "more" in their lives. The hope was and is to connect with men who want to be purposeful in their walk with God and better connect with others, their children, and their spouses.

If we had a theme, it would be the military motto: "Leave no man behind." I believe men were meant to live life in community and together, not alone or in darkness. We need to find ways to get involved socially, whether that be a Bible study at church, a local bowling league, or another hobby group. As such, having a positive brotherhood around you is as important as your attitude on a daily basis. Developing strong, supportive relationships and coping skills allows you to reach your full potential in life.

What is a *True Man*?

To better understand the term, *True Man*, I believe we need to start by asking, "Who is Jesus?" According to the Bible, Jesus Christ is God's Son, the second person of the Holy Trinity, true God, and a True Man.

To change our lives, we need to become aware of the battle for our hearts between good and evil. Becoming a True Man of God means orienting our lives to Jesus's words.

> *"If anyone is confident in himself that they belong to Christ, they should consider again that we belong to Christ just as much as they do."*
> (2 Corinthians 10:7)

True men of God have an intimate walk with Jesus that is seen in their lives. Jesus said, *"You will know them by their fruits"* (Matthew 7:16). A biblical leader understands that Jesus is the son of God who died on a real cross for our sins. Jesus lived a perfect life and gave a perfect sacrifice. Our only hope for salvation rests in the death, burial, and resurrection of Jesus Christ.

So, how do we find the right direction to follow in the footsteps of Jesus Christ? When I originally designed the logo for our *True Man* small group, I chose a compass as an intentional and important clue to what the group of True Man represented. Just as a compass can provide direction, so can an oriented True Man find direction in his life.

A compass's singular purpose is to tell you what direction you are heading in at all times, which prevents you from getting lost. Jesus provided us with this direction as a *True Man* on earth by teaching, witnessing, and providing us with anecdotes on how to live.

But let's face facts: the art of becoming a *True Man* is wrought with distraction, hardship, and even evil.

How do I know about hardship? I am a lifelong Christian and follower of Christ. I thought my faith was growing as I became more active in the church by serving and getting involved. Maybe you have experienced this? However, something was missing, and I knew it. Something was churning deep in my soul. Question after question was coming at me with no way to explain what was happening.

Was I suffering a midlife crisis? Was I burned out with what I was doing? Why did I feel so empty when I had so much around me?

I remember wondering, is there more to life than this? Am I the man I want to be?

Then, I had an opportunity to attend a men's retreat. I had never been on a retreat before, let alone one that featured nearly 300 men. I was skeptical about going but knew the possibility existed that I may learn something about myself and perhaps how I could become closer to God.

On Saturday morning of the retreat, we began worship with a series of songs where we were encouraged to think of the music as God singing them to us.

As the music began, I heard a song that I had never heard before by writer and performer Josh Groban. The song was called "You Are Loved (Never Give Up)."

The words go like this:

Don't give up.
It's just the weight of the world.
When your heart's heavy
I will lift it for you.

Don't give up.
Because you want to be heard.
If silence keeps you
I will break it for you.

Everybody wants to be understood.
Well, I can hear you.
Everybody wants to be loved.
Don't give up because you are loved.

Don't give up.
It's just the hurt that you hide.
When you're lost inside
I'll be there to find you.

Don't give up.
Because you want to burn bright.
If darkness blinds you
I will shine to guide you.

Everybody wants to be understood.
Well, I can hear you.
Everybody wants to be loved.

Don't give up because you are loved.
(You are loved.)
You are loved.
(You are loved.)

What I heard, felt, and saw at that moment was an intimate and loving relationship with Christ unlike any I had known before. At that moment, I heard God say, "You are loved, heard, seen, and understood," and "my beloved Son." In an instant, I knew that my relationship with Christ had changed forever. I finally had the missing piece.

This was the beginning of a true Father-son relationship that I could cultivate and explore for the remainder of my lifetime. I realized that Christ's earthly walk as a *True Man* could be passed on to *all men* on their earthly journeys. By following Jesus's path, you can become a true leader, father, husband, and child of God.

I believe that every man wants to be understood, heard, and loved. And those attributes, combined with a loving relationship with Christ, can help you come alive as a man.

There are many attributes to becoming a *True Man*; by using them, you can begin to walk in the footsteps of Jesus Christ, the ultimate *True Man,* and explore True Ways.

Creating True Ways and True Desires

In your journey to become a *True Man*, it's important to create a plan for attaining your goals. I will talk more specifically about goals in chapter 5, but for now, understand that the attributes described in this book will help you develop a plan and strategy for your life.

Before creating your roadmap to reach your goals, check in with God to ensure it's what He wants for you. Even when you don't see any solution to your problem, God will help you find a way. *"Behold, I will do a new thing; now it shall spring forth; shall ye not know it? I will even make a way in the wilderness, and rivers in the desert."* Isaiah 43:19 (KJV)

If we put our trust in God and let him lead us and develop our plans through prayerful consideration, our chances of success go up dramatically, even if it feels like the "deck is stacked against us."

Jack Canfield says in his book The Success Principles that "we should be 100% responsible for everything going on in our lives. Even if something doesn't seem like it's in our control, we should still take responsibility for it."[15]

I couldn't agree more with this statement. When bad things happen to us, we often point our finger at others instead of realizing that our own choices might be to blame for our unfortunate circumstances. We don't take full responsibility for what we've done because it makes us feel like we've lost control of our lives.

"And Jesus looking upon them saith, With men it is impossible, but not with God: for with God all things are possible." Mark 10:27 (KJV)

Maybe it's time for you to stop gripping the steering wheel so tight! What do you think?

If your goal is to become more like Jesus Christ, then follow "The Way," (as Christ referred to in Acts I and II), and you must also commit to creating your path through Him.

---

[15] Canfield, Jack. "Taking 100% Responsibility for Your Life." Web log. *Jackcanfield.Com* (blog). Jack Canfield. Accessed August 8, 2024. https://jackcanfield.com/blog/taking-100-responsibility-for-your-life/

One way to do this is by creating a step-by-step approach to discovering your true desires. Decide what you want before you receive it; create that vision in your mind. By doing this, the universe can begin to fulfill your deepest desires, but you must first identify what those desires are for yourself. For many, this type of thinking can be difficult.

You may be reluctant to express your desires for fear of appearing ungrateful. When we're raised in a culture that tells us to work hard to get what we want, expecting to express our desires and then be ready to receive them can be difficult. So, how can we be more specific about our desires?

We must first believe that we are deserving of our own happiness. You're looking for the things, people, and situations you believe will help you achieve your ideal life and your happiness. Achieving your ideal life will be nearly impossible if you don't believe you deserve it. If you're having trouble with this, take some time to forgive yourself for the things you think you owe someone. Next, work on creating the life of your dreams.

Then, in each area of your life, write down the things you'd like to have or experience. Home life, work life, relationships, success, and creativity are all examples of this. Each item should have as much detail as possible. Instead of saying, "I want a new job in my life," write down all of the characteristics you're looking for in a new career. Go all the way. Accepting mediocrity is not an option. Make a list of all the qualities you look for in a new employer or career.

Close your eyes and imagine yourself and this job in a scene you've just written down. How do you feel about this job? What does the future look like? Where has this job been all my life? Your true desires can be fulfilled by doing this. When you're in the job of your dreams, you're probably looking for a certain level of satisfaction. What would cause you to feel this way? The more time you spend visualizing your ideal — whatever it is — the more items you will add to your to-do list.

Each area of your life can benefit from this simple exercise. You can open yourself up to receiving your ideal life by visualizing, praying, and getting clear about what you want.

Changing your life's trajectory is possible, but only if you're willing to take responsibility for your own actions. No one else can tell you how to live your life, and no one else can assist you in creating the life you desire either. No one else can help you. You are the master of your destiny, and starting late is preferable to never.

Please don't continue to fall for the common trap that many men fall into. You can continue asking yourself questions and never answering them, or you can begin to develop the ways of a *True Man* and achieve your most important desires.

However, without a deep look into the mirror, or in many cases, the occurrence of a life tragedy or life-changing event, most men will carry questions, wounds, hurts, and pain with them and choose not to take action. This is a mistake, and it usually shows up when you're least expecting or desiring it.

Now it's time to pull over for a rest stop. What do you read or think about on this leg of the trip? Did anything sound familiar to you?

The journey to becoming a True Man rests in two of the most wonderful words ever spoken by Christ; "follow me." These two simple but powerful words lay the groundwork for the rest of our trip.

Scan the code above with your smartphone
to view my chapter wrap-up video.

Go to this link to access the Chapter Worksheets:
https://truemanlifecoaching.com/TrueManTrueWaysWorksheets

Rest Stop

In the following pages, journal and reflect on your thoughts about how you can model and become a True Man. How do you define what a True Man is?

_____

_____

_____

_____

_____

_____

_____

_____

_____

_____

_____

_____

_____

_____

_____

_____

_____

_____

_____

_____

_____

TRUE MAN

Chapter Four

Fueling the Heart and Mind with Emotional Well-Being

True Man Tip

The distance between your heart and head may be mere inches, yet the journey toward healing demands miles of patience, persistence, and unshakeable faith in the knowledge that God holds you in His hands.

Life is a journey filled with challenges and triumphs, and in the pursuit of our goals, we often neglect a crucial aspect — our mental and emotional well-being. In fact, in a man's world, his heart's well-being is missed almost entirely. Why? Our "training" as men almost always causes us to lead with our head versus our heart. It's why when someone says I need help, we default to fixing before asking how we can help.

If you're going to equip yourself for life's adventures and the twists and turns of the road ahead, you must examine your wounds before rushing to save the world.

Chapter 4 explores the importance of nurturing our mental and emotional health. We will also examine the masculine heart and its value. This is not just a chapter; it's a guide to fortifying your inner strength, ensuring you face the world with resilience and balance.

A Man's Wounding

I've heard a lot of men's stories, and most of them have experienced a trauma or an event that left a deep scar. Herein lies the problem: hurt men harm their sons, and those sons grow up to hurt their own families.

Before we can put a roadmap to recovery in place, we must address the "elephant in the room." A man's wounding!

Barna Group, a Christian research firm, recently conducted a survey and found Christian men say masculinity is threatened rather than hopeful (44% vs. 31%) and endangered rather than thriving.[16] This speaks to the fact that men are wounded, and most are not taking action to do something about it.

In the Bible, the chapter 3 of Genesis sets up the whole story of the fall of man by introducing us to the serpent. God sent Satan to earth because of his rebellion against God in heaven (Luke 10:18). Satan came to Eve as a serpent and told the woman that God had not really forbidden the fruit but instead was keeping it from her for her own good (Genesis 3:1–4). Still, as we all know, she ate it and gave some to Adam (Genesis 3:5).

As we study the story of Genesis, we must not overlook Adam's role in it. In Genesis chapter 2, the Lord specifically said to Adam, *"You may surely eat of every tree of the garden, but of the tree of the knowledge of good and evil you shall not eat, for in the day that you eat of it you shall surely die."*

How are we to address this? Adam has specific directions from God but remains silent and acts passively, and when confronted with temptation, he fails to offer Eve guidance when

---

[16] Barna Group, Five Essentials to Engage Today's Men, Barna Group, 2020 https://www.amazon.com/Five-Essentials-Engage-Todays-Men/dp/1945269774

he knows the rules. Adam's passivity changed everything, and as we now know, a perfect world fell into sin.

God wanted Adam to walk alongside him in an unbroken relationship, yet his disobedience caused the world to fall into sin. In an instant, everything changed. This Biblical wound would transcend time and enter the hearts of every man. Just like Adam, men today are scared, bruised, and licking their wounds in isolation.

The story of Adam is important and helps us understand the underlying current that most men swim up against. Below the water surface, men find themselves worried, tired, and frustrated, but they don't want to admit it. Even if they do admit it, being the best professional, father, and husband still feels elusive. Frustrated by the mountains of expectations hoisted upon them, many men fall into passivity. By the time a man reaches midlife, stress levels are high, happiness is low, and trying to figure out the quality of life seems like a fantasy.

This may seem like an obvious statement, but we are all broken people, and we all have something challenging us. Everyone is unique; but, news flash - chances are very high that someone has walked the same path and come out on the other side. This is not to dismiss what you're going through because it may be taking you down a dark hole. When you're in that hole, you're in a fragile state, and you need to address that hurt as quickly as possible, but most men do not.

When I was growing up, I thought the only thing that mattered was sports. I guess, in some ways, I still want to believe that. When my teams lost, I thought the world was ending, and I didn't take it well, and I didn't take it lightly. To me, being on the field or the court was the ultimate battlefield, and when I was on it, time stood still. It's safe to say that when I was in the classroom, the total opposite was true. The only battlefield was in my mind, waiting for the 3:00 bell to chime so I could get to practice.

I don't think there is any doubt that we all need a mission in life. I fought the hardest for wins, but the problem was I lost much more than I won. This leads to another problem men face. You can't get through life being a sore loser. If winning versus effort becomes our primary driver, and you lose more often than you win, it can take a toll on your attitude, your confidence, and your motivation. Remember that your losses do not reflect on who you are as a man. Take each disappointment as an opportunity; after all, you learn more from your failures than from your successes.

Ultimately, I would pay a price for my bad study habits as an adult. I bounced from job to job, and I found myself searching for something elusive that I couldn't put my hands on. When you're feeling lost, it's very easy to sabotage your mind and ignore your heart. As men, we do this well.

Have you experienced this?

Self-sabotage is something many people go through. It can be a horrible feeling to realize that you messed up in life at a young age when you just wanted to succeed at everything you did. Most self-defeating behavior happens when you are unhappy, and it can spiral quickly. No one wants to fail or lose, but the pain of those moments is where opportunity emerges, if you're ready.

Have you felt this?

In life, there is no guarantee of success, but when you're young, it's hard to convince yourself of that. In my unfortunate experience, I was so ashamed of my failures that I made a lot of bad decisions. I was spiritually wounded, which led me to feeling lost and out of control.

Many men go through much worse trauma than I did. These traumas ultimately sabotage positive thinking and lead to a life of searching for answers. These traumas range from divorce, to physical and sexual abuse, to the deep wounds left by war, and so on. These events build up in men, like stacking bricks on top of bricks.

These layers of bricks become the secret wounds that men carry around. Just like building a foundation, the layers of hurt build and can become immense, and one secret can lead toward another and on and on. The idea that "real men" are tough enough to endure past hurts or wounds is false thinking. There is no badge of honor for trying to tough it out, especially when you leave a trail of debris behind you.

When it comes to working on past hurts, being mindful of your emotions helps you to process your trauma. Is it weak to not show your emotion? Certainly not; expressing emotions and being vulnerable is an exercise in courage and bravery, not weakness. Men are good at keeping their problems and sorrows hidden from everybody, but that rarely works out well and usually creates other bad habits.

What are some of the things holding men back?

Here are four problems that I often hear from men:

1. **Fear of losing control if we express our feelings**. Many men worry that sharing their innermost thoughts and emotions with others will end badly. One of the more effective things I've done is to find people that I trust enough to share openly with. Who are trustworthy people? People I can be vulnerable with, so the smell of fear is not as strong. There is nothing better than being able to shoot straight with people who hold you accountable and

push you to be your best. Getting involved in a men's group is a great way to accomplish this.

2. **Lack of an emotionally grounded male role model.** Many men have never had a positive male role model to help show them how to express emotions. Their fathers, grandparents, coaches, and other authority figures likely passed on what they had learned themselves: that real men don't show vulnerability. We model what we see, hear, and what we are taught.

3. **Powerful cultural influences that teach violence over vulnerability.** Let's face it: we have a culture that glorifies a specific idea of masculinity: a powerful, muscular hero who never cries. Think Rambo, Rocky, Gladiator, or the Terminator. These men don't show weakness or vulnerability with anyone except their female love interest. As a counterpoint, think of Jesus and how he modeled love and tenderness to others.

4. **Not wanting to appear feminine or weak**. On the flip side of manly men is the fear of coming across as "feminine." Men worry that showing vulnerability will reflect on their masculinity. The fact is, to some degree or another, we all have a balance of masculine and feminine qualities.

My pursuit in this book isn't to dive into a psychological cure for everything a man goes through. I'm not the least bit qualified to do that, but what I hope to do is bring awareness to the fact you're not alone in how you feel or what you've gone through, regardless of what it is. Many men isolate themselves and believe the wounds of their past may not be fixable, or perhaps they just don't want to deal with them. I don't encourage any of that. It doesn't typically work out well or at all.

As I've learned to do, scripture provides us guidance on where to turn to in times of trouble. Roman 5:3-5 KJV reads, "And not only so, but we glory in tribulations also: knowing that tribulations worketh patience. And patience, experience; and experience, hope. And hope maketh not ashamed; because the love of God is shed abroad in our hearts by the Holy Ghost which is given unto us."

With that, let's look at healing and where that starts.

Scan the code above with your smartphone
to view my chapter wrap-up video.

Go to this link to access the Chapter Worksheets:
https://truemanlifecoaching.com/TrueManTrueWaysWorksheets

Rest Stop

In the following pages, journal and reflect on the wounds that have held you back in life and how you feel you can begin to overcome them.

_____

_____

_____

_____

_____

_____

_____

_____

_____

_____

_____

_____

_____

_____

_____

_____

_____

_____

TRUE MAN

Chapter Five

The Heart

True Man Tip

When a man looks within his heart and sees what is good and right, connecting it II to the love of Christ, he can begin to seek the freedom and authenticity he desires.

Did you know that the body carries 60,000 miles of blood vessels?[17] In context, it is approximately 3,000 miles across the United States from the west coast to the east coast. If you hopped in a car and drove back and forth roundtrip, that would be a heck of a road trip, and you would do it 10 times. Just stop and think about what God created, but wait, there's more.

For many years, scientists believed that pain is created in the brain. However, pain is also related to emotional, cognitive, and social components. If you've ever lost a loved one or someone you're close to, you've probably felt that deep pain in your chest.

Scientists have discovered that the heart acts as a "little brain" or "intrinsic cardiac nervous system." The "heart brain" has approximately 40,000 nerve cells, similar to brain cells.[18] This means

---

[17] "Functions of Blood: Transport around the Body." NHS Blood Donation. Accessed August 8, 2024. https://www.blood.co.uk/news-and-campaigns/the-donor/latest-stories/functions-of-blood-transport-around-the-body/

[18] Alshami, Ali M. "Pain: Is It All in the Brain or the Heart?" *Current pain and headache reports* vol. 23,12 88. 14 Nov. 2019, doi:10.1007/s11916-019-0827-4

that the heart has its own nervous system. Also, the heart and brain talk to each other in many ways, including through nerves, biochemistry, physics, and energy. The vagus nerve sends information from the heart and other organs inside the body to the brain.[19] The heart talks to the brain more than the brain talks to the heart. The heart is likely a key moderator of pain.

Let's look at the heart from a faith perspective. In the King James version of the Bible, the term "heart" is cited 826 times, while "brain" is mentioned once. God challenged us to focus on what really matters: our hearts.

"But the Lord said unto Samuel, Look not on his countenance, or on the height of his stature; because I have refused him: for the Lord seeth not as man seeth; for man looketh on the outward appearance, but the Lord looketh on the heart." 1 Samuel 16:7 KJV

Saul was the most attractive man in Israel, and for a season, God blessed his kingly rule. Over time, Saul disobeyed God's word and started slaughtering priests. So, God sent Samuel once again to anoint another king, a godly leader for His chosen people.

God led Samuel to Jesse of Bethlehem, who had several sons. One in particular, Abinadab, who was strong and good-looking, caught Samuel's eye as a potential choice. But God said, "No, the Lord looks on the heart." Finally, Jesse's youngest son, David, a most unlikely choice, was brought before Samuel and chosen as Israel's future king. From David's line would come Jesus, our Savior, the One who would save us from sin and eternal death.

---

[19] https://pmc.ncbi.nlm.nih.gov/articles/PMC10896837/

God looks at our hearts. He is not impressed by our physical appearance and abilities because Jesus resides in our hearts, and it is from our hearts that his love shines forth to others.

Wow, I hope that comes as a relief for many of you. As men, this tells us that we need to make more decisions with our hearts and fewer with our heads. It also tells us we need to heal our heart from past wounds and transgressions that have a tendency to hold us back.

Admittedly, I haven't always done the best job investing time in my heart. What I've come to realize is, the only thing I should be investing my time in is my heart. Why haven't I done this? It's uncomfortable, it creates uncertainty, and I don't always see or hear God in the middle of it. There is also the question of what happens if I discover a wound or a trauma. What should I do? How do I deal with it? How could it affect my head and my heart?

Have you ever asked yourself those questions?

The funny thing is that Scripture tells us that God's Spirit lives in our hearts. *"That Christ may dwell in your hearts by faith; that ye, being rooted and grounded in love."* Ephesians 3:17 KJV It's great news to know that God lives in our hearts, but what about the wounded heart? What do we do with that?

Wounded Hearts

The human heart is resilient and can endure immense joy and profound pain. For men, societal expectations often encourage them to suppress emotions and toughen up, leading to unresolved wounds that can linger for a lifetime. However, healing is possible, and addressing these wounds is essential for overall well-being.

Before diving into the healing process, it's crucial to understand the nature of the wounds that may have accumulated over a lifetime. These wounds can stem from various sources, such as childhood trauma, broken relationships, societal pressures, or personal failures. They manifest differently in each individual, often leaving emotional scars, insecurities, or self-limiting beliefs. Suppressing past traumas can have far-reaching adverse effects on a man's life, from his mental and emotional well-being to his relationships and overall quality of life.

How do these traumas and wounds show up?

The psychological effects can produce several challenges. Suppressed emotions and traumas can manifest in various psychological issues, such as:

- anxiety
- depression
- low self-esteem
- post-traumatic stress disorder (PTSD)
- emotional numbness
- frequent mood swings
- outbursts of anger or sadness
- a general sense of emotional detachment
- difficulty in forming and maintaining healthy personal and professional relationships.

These wounds can also affect your physical health. Chronic stress (from PTSD or other emotional issues) may weaken the immune system, increase the risk of cardiovascular problems, and contribute to other stress-related ailments.[20]

To cope with past wounds and traumas, some men may resort to escapist behaviors. These coping mechanisms might include:

---

[20] Coughlin, Steven S. "Post-traumatic Stress Disorder and Cardiovascular Disease." *The open cardiovascular medicine journal* vol. 5 (2011): 164-70. doi:10.2174/1874192401105010164

- substance abuse (alcohol, drugs)
- excessive gambling
- pornography
- other addictive behaviors

Unfortunately, these addictive behaviors only mask the pain; over time, they compound and create larger problems.

Even when you think you've overcome your issues, those past hurts don't disappear. They will resurface in other ways, such as self-isolation, reckless behavior, relationship problems, anger issues, or even self-harm. All of these will limit growth and fulfillment, causing a man to feel stuck or unable to pursue their goals and aspirations due to unresolved emotional baggage holding them back.

The first step towards healing is acknowledging the existence of these wounds and accepting them without judgment. Many men are taught to bury their pain, viewing it as a sign of weakness. However, true strength lies in true vulnerability. By acknowledging the pain, men can begin to reclaim their power and take control of their emotional well-being. Is this easy?

Absolutely not! Ignoring your past pains seems easier than confronting them. But when men do this, they retreat into darkness instead of facing their problems head-on. But there is hope. Seeking support from mental health professionals or trusted coaches can be crucial in processing and healing from these experiences. When your heart is broken or hurting, God can provide some relief.

"He healeth the broken in heart, and bindeth up their wounds." Psalm 147:3 KJV

"The Lord is nigh unto them that are of the broken heart, and saveth such as be of contrite spirit." Psalm 34:18 KJV

"Peace I leave with you, my peace I give unto you: not as the world giveth, give I unto you. Let not your heart be troubled, neither let it be afraid." John 14:27 KJV

Men, stop complicating the obvious. Yes, I'm looking in the mirror as I say this. God has given us the answers and the roadmap and solved the problem of taking care of our hearts. The only question is, will you submit to his will?

Healing Hearts

First and foremost, you must release control and let God take the wheel. Submitting to God's will has been a focal point of my prayers and self-exploration. The human tendency is to seek control, and when it slips away, we grapple with discomfort, vulnerability, and anxiety about the uncertainties of life. It can be akin to losing one's breath or experiencing a pause in the heart's rhythm.

In 2014, singer Danny Gokey released a song called "Tell Your Heart to Beat Again." The lyrics tell the story of someone who has experienced heartbreak and loss. The song encourages the listener to find strength in the face of adversity, to let go of the past, and to embrace a new beginning. It conveys a message of hope, healing, and renewal. Even in moments of despair, healing and moving forward is possible.

Healing begins by acknowledging the existence of old wounds and accepting them without judgment. By embracing vulnerability, you can cultivate deeper relationships with yourself and others, fostering a sense of belonging and acceptance.

Speaking of belonging, I want to remind you that healing is not a solitary journey; seeking support from trusted friends, family members, or professionals can be invaluable. Men often struggle with opening up about their feelings, because they fear judgment or rejection. However, authentic connections and compassionate listening can provide a safe space for healing to occur. Whether through therapy, support groups, or simply heartfelt conversations, reaching out for a helping hand is a courageous step toward healing.

The foundation of this book is rooted in my experiences within the True Man small group. The significance of cultivating genuine connections and support through participation in a men's small group cannot be overstated. I advocate for the concept of discovering your community of men. Genuine healing unfolds as you engage and gain wisdom from fellow men, fostering warm and authentic conversations that guide you toward embodying the True Man you aspire to be.

Outside of the importance of men's groups, healing the heart requires self-compassion and forgiveness, both towards yourself and others. Many men carry guilt, shame, or resentment from past experiences, which can weigh heavily on the heart. Practicing self-compassion involves treating yourself with kindness and understanding and acknowledging that mistakes are a natural part of the human experience. Similarly, forgiveness is not about condoning hurtful actions but releasing the burden of resentment and moving forward with a lighter heart.

There are many ways to lighten the load on your heart; mindfulness, and self-reflection are powerful tools for doing that. By cultivating present-moment awareness, you can observe your thoughts and emotions without judgment, gaining clarity and insight into your inner world. Self-reflection allows for deeper exploration of past wounds, patterns, and triggers, enabling men to develop greater self-awareness and make conscious choices aligned with their values and desires. (See chapter two on journaling and use this mindfulness and self-reflection as an invitation to get thoughts on paper and in writing).

Healing requires letting go of the need to control outcomes and surrendering to the natural flow of life. Many men cling to rigid expectations and resist change, feeling uncertain and vulnerable. However, true freedom lies in surrendering to the present moment and trusting in the inherent wisdom of life's unfolding. By relinquishing control and embracing the unknown, men can experience a profound sense of liberation and peace within their hearts.

Finally, healing the heart is a journey of self-discovery, courage, and compassion. For men, addressing lifelong wounds requires a willingness to confront vulnerability, seek support, and cultivate self-awareness and acceptance. By acknowledging their pain, embracing vulnerability, and practicing self-compassion, men can reclaim their power and create a life filled with authenticity, connection, and joy. Remember, healing is not a destination but a continuous process of growth and transformation guided by the wisdom of the heart.

Masculinity and Mental Health Stigma

It is often mentioned that the distance from the heart to the brain ranges from 12 to 14 inches, depending on an individual's height. I am convinced that recognizing the pivotal role of the heart in both causing wounds and facilitating healing is essential, but we must also address the complexities of mental health.

In the world of mental health, an intricate web of societal expectations, gender norms, and cultural perceptions often inter-twine to create a complex landscape. Nowhere is this complex-ity more evident than in the stigma surrounding mental health issues, particularly among men. In a world where traditional masculinity often emphasizes stoicism, strength, and self-reli-ance, seeking help for mental health concerns can be seen as a sign of weakness. This stigma not only affects individual men but also perpetuates a cycle of silence and suffering that undermines their well-being and hinders progress toward a more inclusive and understanding society.

From a young age, many boys are taught to suppress their emotions and adopt a façade of toughness. Phrases like "boys don't cry" or "man up" reinforce the idea that expressing vulnerability is opposing to masculinity. This pressure to conform to traditional gender roles can have profound implications for mental health. Men may feel compelled to hide their struggles, fearing that admitting to emotional distress will make them appear inadequate or emasculated in the eyes of others.

Has this type of teaching hindered your development?

Additionally, societal expectations often dictate that men should be the providers, the protectors, and the problem-solvers. Admitting to mental health challenges may be perceived as a failure to fulfill these roles, further exacerbating feelings of shame and inadequacy. As a result, many men suffer in silence, reluctant to seek support or treatment for fear of judgment or ridicule.

The stigma surrounding mental health not only affects how men perceive themselves but also influences how others view and interact with them. Stereotypes about masculinity may lead friends, family members, or even healthcare providers to overlook or downplay symptoms of mental illness in men. Consequently, men may struggle to receive the help and support they need, leading to a worsening of their condition over time.

The fear of being stigmatized may prevent men from opening up about their experiences, even to those closest to them. Closing yourself off from others can deepen feelings of loneliness and despair, which, in turn, exacerbate mental health issues and increase the risk of suicide. Indeed, statistics show that men are less likely than women to seek professional help for mental health problems. A 2019 study showed that 24.7% of women sought treatment for their mental health compared to just 13.4% of men.[21] Men are also disproportionately affected by suicide.[22]

Breaking the stigma surrounding mental health and masculinity requires a multifaceted approach that addresses both individual attitudes and societal norms. First, we must challenge the notion that vulnerability is synonymous with weakness. True strength lies in the courage to confront our struggles and seek help when needed. By reframing the narrative around masculinity to include emotional expression and vulnerability, we can create a more inclusive and compassionate definition of what it means to be a man.

Education also plays a crucial role in dismantling stigma. By raising awareness about the prevalence of mental health issues among men and debunking myths about masculinity, we can encourage open conversations and foster a greater sense of understanding and empathy. Schools, workplaces, and communities can implement programs aimed at promoting mental health literacy and providing resources for those in need.

Normalizing these mental health discussions is the antidote to this toxic stigma. By openly talking about our mental well-being, we dismantle the walls that confine those struggling in silence. It's about creating a space where sharing your mental health journey is as natural as discussing physical ailments.

[21] Terlizzi, Emily P. and Zablotsky, Benjamin. "Mental Health Treatment Among Adults: United States, 2019." CDC.gov. CDC, September 2020. Accessed August 8, 2024. https://www.cdc.gov/nchs/products/databriefs/db380.htm

[22] Sagar-Ouriaghli, Ilyas et al. "Improving Mental Health Service Utilization Among Men: A Systematic Review and Synthesis of Behavior Change Techniques Within Interventions Targeting Help-Seeking." *American journal of men's health* vol. 13,3 (2019): 1557988319857009. doi:10.1177/1557988319857009

How would a safe space to talk about your journey help prevent you from struggling in silence?

I'm writing this book to empower men to speak up about mental health issues or traumas we bury in our souls. Men who have the courage to speak out about their own experiences with mental illness can serve as powerful role models, demonstrating that seeking help is not a sign of inadequacy, but a testament to resilience and self-awareness. By sharing their stories, these individuals can inspire others to break free from the shackles of stigma and embrace their mental health journey with honesty and authenticity.

Ultimately, breaking the stigma surrounding mental health and masculinity requires a collective effort from individuals, communities, and institutions alike. By challenging outdated stereotypes, promoting education and awareness, and creating supportive environments, we can empower men to prioritize their mental well-being and seek help without fear or shame. Together, we can build a more compassionate society where everyone feels valued, supported, and understood.

The Path to Healing: Developing Self-Awareness and Emotional Intelligence

Whether talking about the heart, mental health, or the wounds and traumas that shape us, self-awareness and emotional intelligence combined with faith can lead us toward healing. The path to healing and emotional intelligence is not a journey for the faint-hearted; it demands an unwavering commitment from men to confront the shadows that linger within.

To traverse this transformative terrain, a man must first acknowledge the existence of his emotional landscape and understand that strength lies not just in the muscles that sculpt his physique but in the depth of his self-awareness. The key to unlocking emotional well-being begins with a fearless excavation of your heart.

This excavation necessitates a departure from the stoic façade you've used like armor so that you may embrace your trauma and vulnerability. This is the gateway to profound healing.

Self-awareness is the cornerstone of emotional intelligence. It requires a conscious effort to dissect the layers of one's emotional core, examining the scars that time has etched upon it. To embark on this odyssey, you must confront the discomfort often accompanying introspection. It demands a deliberate commitment to peel back the layers, uncovering the triumphs and wounds beneath. This process is an act of courage and a testament to the strength required to face your inner demons. In this exploration, you will discover the intricate details of your emotions, woven with threads of joy, pain, love, and sorrow. The shadows that once seemed daunting dissipate as the light of self-awareness illuminates the path to healing.

Healing, however, is not a passive endeavor; it is an active and intentional pursuit. You must be willing to confront the darkness head-on, armed not with stoicism but with the vulnerability that comes from acknowledging your humanity. If you're willing to do the hard work, you can heal the scars of past pain, whether they are from a turbulent childhood, war, or another traumatic event. Healing requires seeking support from trusted friends, mentors, or mental health professionals. It demands the humility to accept that strength is not measured by the ability to bear burdens alone but by the courage to share the load with others.

In the realm of emotional intelligence, empathy becomes the compass guiding you through the terrain of human connection. The ability to resonate with the emotions of others without losing sight of your own is a strength you can develop.

Developing empathy involves transcending the boundaries of your perspective, stepping into the shoes of another, and understanding their journey.

It is an active engagement with the world, a conscious effort to listen, comprehend, feel, and connect. In forging these empathetic connections, you broaden your understanding of the human experience and discover the profound impact of genuine connection on the road to recovery.

In addition, cultivating emotional intelligence requires honing communication skills to express what we feel honestly and connect deeply with others. True strength lies not in silence but in articulating your thoughts and emotions. This requires an ongoing dialogue with oneself, a practice of introspection that finds expression in open and honest communication with others.

The ability to convey one's feelings, needs, and boundaries fosters healthier relationships and allows for a deeper connection with oneself. By mastering communication, you can become the architect of your own emotional landscape, building bridges of understanding and dismantling the walls that hinder authentic connection.

The Power of Mindfulness, Emotional Intelligence, and Resiliency

To embark on this transformative journey, you must embrace the power of mindfulness. It is a practice that anchors the mind in the present moment, allowing for a conscious observation of thoughts and emotions without judgment. Mindfulness provides the space to untangle oneself from the web of past traumas and future anxieties, fostering a sense of clarity and peace. Through the cultivation of mindfulness, you can master your reactions and respond to life's challenges with a calm and centered demeanor. This practice becomes a sanctuary for self-discovery, a refuge where you can weather the storms of life with resilience and grace.

In the quest for emotional intelligence, pursuing your passions becomes a catalyst for personal growth. You can discover your true essence by identifying and nurturing the pursuits that ignite your soul. Passion becomes a conduit for emotional expression and self-discovery, whether in the arts, sports, or intellectual pursuits. Indeed, reconnecting with your true self allows you to propel yourself past the boundaries of societal expectations to tap into the wellspring of your emotions, which may refuel your creativity. This is your sanctuary, where your heart can speak freely, and your soul can soar.

As you traverse the maze of emotional intelligence, you must recognize the importance of resilience in adversity. Life's challenges are inevitable, and the healing journey is not linear. Resilience is not about avoiding pain but embracing it with a spirit that refuses to be broken. It is the unwavering commitment to rise, healthier and wiser, from the ashes of adversity.

This journey demands the cultivation of mindfulness, the pursuit of passion, and the resilience to weather life's storms. Remember, societal expectations and outdated notions of masculinity do not define you. Instead, think about how you can embody a masculinity that is dynamic, compassionate, and resilient. The culmination of this transformative journey is the emergence of a man who stands firmly rooted in his emotional intelligence, a beacon of strength and authenticity.

The path to emotional intelligence for men is a formidable but rewarding journey. It requires a commitment to self-awareness, a willingness to confront past traumas with vulnerability, and the courage to build authentic connections through empathy and communication. If you foster emotional intelligence, you can navigate the intricacies of relationships with grace and form the connections you long for.

In embracing these principles, a man not only heals from the darkness of his past but emerges as a beacon of strength, embodying a masculinity rooted in authenticity and emotional intelligence. This transformative journey is a testament to the power of the human spirit to transcend the shadows and step into the light of profound healing.

As I mentioned earlier, the length from the heart to the brain is 12 to 14 inches, depending on the person's height. However, the healing between the two can feel like a road trip from California to Maine. It can be the most profound journey of your life. Yes, there may be pain, but in that pain, there is also healing. The good news is that Jesus bore that pain with His body on the cross so we may live with the trust of His salvation.

"Who his own self bares our sins in his own body on the tree, that we, being dead to sins, should live unto righteousness: by whose stripes ye were healed."
1 Peter 2:24 KJV

Scan the code above with your smartphone
to view my chapter wrap-up video.

Go to this link to access the Chapter Worksheets:
https://truemanlifecoaching.com/TrueManTrueWaysWorksheets

Rest Stop

In the following pages, journal and reflect on your heart. How can you begin to connect more with your heart and emotions to become the True Man you want to be?

_____

_____

_____

_____

_____

_____

_____

_____

_____

_____

_____

_____

_____

_____

_____

_____

_____

_____

_____

_____

_____

Chapter Six

Setting Goals:
The Dashboard of Life

True Man Tip

Embrace boundless dreams fueled by unwavering persistence. Meaningful goals and relentless vision are the cornerstones of true success. Never settle for playing small.

Life without well-defined goals is like taking a road trip without a map or a clear idea of your destination. You drive aimlessly, feeling out of control, overwhelmed, and afraid of where your path might lead. But fear not; goal-setting provides a beacon of hope — a powerful tool to navigate life's uncertainties and carve out your path to success.

Think of a car's dashboard as a metaphor for goal-setting. The dashboard serves as a vital tool for monitoring and managing the car's performance, the indicators provide crucial information such as speed, fuel level, and engine temperature, allowing the driver to assess the car's current state. Setting clear goals enables you to evaluate your progress, and provides a sense of clarity, direction, and purpose.

In addition, the dashboard alerts the driver to potential issues or hazards, such as low fuel or engine problems, prompting action to address them promptly. Similarly, when pursuing goals, encountering obstacles or setbacks serves as a signal to reassess your approach and make necessary adjustments to stay on course. The odometer allows you to track the distance traveled and the milestones achieved. Tracking your progress allows you to celebrate achievements along the way and motivates you to keep pushing forward.

The dashboard warning lights or alarms alert the driver to immediate dangers, urging swift action to avoid accidents or damage. Pay attention to the hazards on life's path, and you can recognize when we're veering off course or facing imminent risks, prompting decisive action to mitigate them.

In essence, just as the dashboard empowers the driver to navigate the road safely and efficiently, setting and achieving goals empowers us to navigate life with purpose and intention, ensuring we reach our desired destinations while overcoming challenges along the way.

Everyone needs direction, a purpose that ignites your soul and propels you forward. Without clear objectives, you wander aimlessly, lost in uncertainty and indecision. But armed with the power of clearly defined goals, you can chart a course through the wilderness of life, confident in your ability to navigate the twists and turns ahead.

SMART Goals Provide the Map and the Destination

Let's prepare yourselves for a journey into the heart of masculine ambition. Together, we'll unlock the secret to transforming our lives from mere existence into epic adventures filled with purpose, passion, and unbridled success. It's time to unleash the full potential of our masculinity and seize the life we were meant to live through intentional goal-setting.

The art of purposeful goal setting is a skill that separates the men who merely exist from those who truly thrive. The research bears this out. A study conducted by Dr. Gail Matthews, a psychology professor at the Dominican University of California, revealed that jotting down your goals increases the likelihood of achieving them by 42%.[23] Furthermore, there is a clear-cut approach that helps you achieve your intentions by breaking them down into manageable tasks. This is called SMART goals.[24]

SMART stands for:

- Specific
- Measurable
- Achievable
- Relevant
- Time-bound

Breaking down these goals into manageable tasks isn't just a suggestion; it's a game-changer. Imagine rebuilding an old car without the vehicle frame (or chassis) that serves as every car's foundation. You'd only have random car parts without it. It's the same with our ambitions — we must break them down into bite-sized chunks, allowing us to tackle them one step at a time. By doing so, we transform our dreams into achievable milestones, each victory propelling us closer to our ultimate destination.

If SMART goals are the vehicle frame, accountability, and adaptability are the fuel that keeps our engines roaring. Accountability holds us to our word, ensuring we stay true to our commitments even when the going gets tough. Adaptability allows us to

[23] "Study Focuses on Strategies for Achieving Goals, Resolutions." *Dominican.Edu*. Dominican University of California, February 1, 2015. Dominican University of California. https://scholar.dominican.edu/cgi/viewcontent.cgi?article=1265&context=news-releases

[24] Jiménez, Gina. "Slipping on Your New Year's Resolutions? Science Tips to Get on Track." *Scientific American*. Scientific American, January 22, 2024. https://www.scientificamerican.com/article/slipping-on-your-new-years-resolutions-science-tips-to-get-on-track/

pivot and adjust our course as the winds of change blow us off course. Together, they form the backbone of resilience, the trait that separates the men who crumble under pressure from those who rise to the occasion.

How to Create Your Own SMART Goals

S stands for Specific.

Specificity is the cornerstone of effective goal-setting. It's about painting a vivid picture of your goal, leaving no room for ambiguity or vagueness. Instead of saying, "I want to be successful," you must define precisely what success means to you. Is it landing your dream job, launching a successful business, or achieving financial freedom? You set a clear course toward your desired destination by clarifying your objectives.

M stands for Measurable.

Measurability is the compass that guides your progress along this journey. With quantifiable metrics to track your advancement, it's easier to gauge whether you're on track or veering off course. Whether tracking sales numbers, recording daily exercise minutes, or monitoring savings growth, measurable goals provide tangible evidence of your accomplishments and motivate you.

A stands for Achievable.

Achievability is the anchor that keeps your goals grounded in reality. While it's essential to dream big, setting unrealistic objectives can set you up for disappointment and disillusionment. Given your current resources, skills, and circumstances, ensure your goals are attainable. Break down large goals into smaller, more manageable steps, allowing you to build momentum and confidence as you progress.

What does it mean to set an achievable goal? Imagine you want to run a marathon. Rather than jumping in and expecting to run 26.2 miles on your first attempt, you'd set up a realistic plan that breaks this ambitious goal into smaller, manageable steps. Each week, you'd gradually increase your running distance and incorporate cross-training to build stamina and prevent injuries, making your progress steady and attainable.

Starting with a 5K, you'd move toward running a half-marathon within six months. Each milestone adds to your confidence and physical conditioning, setting you up for the ultimate goal of completing a full marathon. By creating clear, incremental steps, you maintain momentum and stay motivated, progressing in a way that keeps you grounded and on track toward your goal of completing a marathon.

R stands for Relevance.
Relativity is like the GPS that charts the entire course of your journey. Consider the big picture of what you want to achieve, and ask yourself, why? Do your objectives contribute to your overall growth and well-being or merely serve as distractions? Ensure your goals align with your values, priorities, and long-term aspirations. Avoid pursuing goals simply because others expect them from you. Stay true to yourself and focus on what matters to you.

T stands for Time-bound.
Time-boundness is the clock that keeps you on schedule. Without a deadline, goals can linger indefinitely, lost in the whirlwind of daily life. Assigning a specific timeframe to each objective creates a sense of urgency and accountability, propelling you toward action and results.

Let's take a deeper look at the SMART formula. When your goals have these characteristics, you are much likelier to achieve them.

Specific

Specificity is the fuel that ignites the engine of achievement. It's the difference between shooting blindly into the dark and taking aim with unwavering precision. When you define your goals with laser-like clarity, you sharpen your focus and illuminate the path ahead.

Gone are vague aspirations like "I want to be successful." Instead, you delve deep into the heart of your desires and articulate your ambitions with surgical precision.

Ask yourself the tough questions:

- What exactly do I want to achieve?
- Who else is involved in this journey?
- What resources do I need?
- When and where will this grand vision unfold?

By answering these questions, you don't just create a roadmap; you sculpt a masterpiece — a crystal-clear vision that serves as your guiding star through life's tumultuous seas. With every detail meticulously laid out, you gain unparalleled clarity, knowing your precise destination and how to get there. For in the clarity of your vision lies the key to unlocking your full potential and charting a course toward the life of your dreams.

Measurable

Imagine embarking on a country-wide road trip without landmarks or milestones to mark your progress. You may end up in an unrecognizable place far from your intended destination. Measurability is the compass that guides your journey towards success. Without it, you're navigating in the dark, unsure of whether you're veering off course, or making progress.

Incorporating quantifiable metrics into your objectives is the key to shedding light on your path and keeping you on track.

Measurable goals allow you to track your progress with precision. You no longer have to rely on guesswork or gut feelings; instead, you have concrete data to guide your decisions and actions. They change the game by providing tangible evidence of your accomplishments.

Here are some examples of setting measurable goals:

- Tracking sales numbers provides insight into the effectiveness of your strategies, helping you identify areas for improvement and doubling down on what works.
- Recording daily exercise minutes allows you to monitor your fitness journey, celebrate milestones, and push yourself to new heights.
- Monitoring savings growth empowers you to take control of your financial future, inching closer to your long-term goals with each deposit.

If you embrace quantifiable metrics as your allies, you can use them to track your progress, celebrate your victories, and stay motivated along the way. Assessing your progress tells you if you are on a path to success.

Achievable

Achievability grounds your aspirations in the realm of possibility rather than fantasy. While it's admirable to dream big and reach for the stars, setting goals beyond your grasp can lead to frustration and disillusionment. It can undermine your confidence and motivation and set you up for failure. Instead, focus on setting objectives that are within reach by asking yourself if you have the tools to accomplish them.

Before committing to a goal, do the following:

- Take stock of your strengths and limitations; is your goal reasonable?

- Consider your resources and life circumstances. Do you have the time and money to make your dream happen?
- Evaluate if you have the necessary skills, knowledge, and support to reach your aims.
- Remember, it's not about settling for mediocrity but rather about setting yourself up for success.

Break down large goals into smaller, more manageable steps, like laying bricks to build a fortress. By breaking the journey into bite-sized tasks, you create a roadmap that guides you through the wilderness of uncertainty. Each small victory is a building block, propelling you forward with renewed momentum and confidence.

Every step forward, no matter how small, brings you closer to your ultimate destination. Celebrate these victories along the way, no matter how insignificant. Whether it's completing a task ahead of schedule, overcoming a challenge, or mastering a new skill, take time to acknowledge your progress and pat yourself on the back.

Remember, Rome wasn't built in a day, and neither are your goals. The consistent effort and dedication you put into each step of the journey lead to success. So, gentlemen, set your sights high, but keep your feet firmly planted on the ground. Setting achievable goals and celebrating every milestone will pave the way for a future filled with triumph and fulfillment.

Relevant

Relevance is the GPS that keeps you on course, guiding your goals toward alignment with your deepest values and aspirations. In a world full of distractions and external pressures, staying true to yourself and pursuing objectives that resonate with your core beliefs and priorities is essential.

Before committing to a goal, take a moment to reflect on its significance in the grand tapestry of your life.

Ask yourself:

- Does this goal align with values, passions, and long-term aspirations?
- How will it contribute to your overall growth and well-being in the short and long term?

Avoid pursuing goals simply because they're trendy or because others expect you to. Remember, it's not about keeping up with the Joneses; it's about honoring your values and staying true to your vision for your life. True success isn't about chasing after someone else's definition of happiness; it's about forging your path and living authentically. Stay grounded in what truly matters to you, whether that's building meaningful relationships, pursuing a passion project, or positively impacting your community.

Let relevance be your guiding star as you set out on your goal-setting journey. Choose objectives that resonate with your soul, align with your values, and bring you one step closer to the life of your dreams. In doing so, you'll achieve success and find meaning and purpose along the way.

Time-bound

Assigning a timeline to your goals serves as the clock that keeps you on track. Without a specific finishing date, goals languish in uncertainty, at the mercy of the whims of daily life. Remembering that you have a deadline helps to drive your progress by injecting a sense of urgency and purpose into your endeavors.

Imagine embarking on a journey without a destination or a map, aimlessly wandering through the wilderness with no end in sight. That's the reality of setting goals without a deadline — a recipe for stagnation and frustration. But with a clear timeframe in place, you create a sense of urgency that fuels your determination and propels you towards action.

Whether it's a daily, weekly, monthly, or yearly deadline, time-bound goals provide structure and direction, guiding your efforts with unwavering purpose. Each deadline becomes a milestone, marking your progress and signaling your commitment to achieving your objectives.

Time-bound goals are more than just markers on a calendar; they're powerful motivators that keep you focused and driven. As the deadline looms closer, you feel a sense of urgency that pushes you to take action and make progress toward your goal. It's this sense of impending deadline that spurs you into action, driving you forward with unwavering determination.

In the whirlwind of daily life, it's easy to lose sight of our goals amidst the chaos of competing priorities and distractions. However, time-bound goals serve as a beacon of clarity, guiding our actions and decisions with precision. With each deadline, we're reminded of the importance of staying focused and disciplined, even in the face of adversity.

As you set out on your goal-setting journey, remember the power of time-bound goals. Assign specific deadlines to each objective, creating a sense of urgency and accountability that propels you towards action and results. By harnessing the power of time, you'll transform your dreams into reality, one deadline at a time.

Putting SMART Goals Together

Now that we've explored the essence of SMART goals, let's discuss the importance of breaking them into manageable tasks. While setting ambitious objectives is admirable, it can make you feel overwhelmed and out of control. However, deconstructing your goals into bite-sized tasks creates a clear roadmap for success. Maintaining momentum and staying on track on your journey requires discipline, accountability, and resilience. Creating a system for accountability and tracking progress will help you stay on track.

Tips to help you stay accountable:

- Share your goals with a trusted friend
- Join a small group, such as a mastermind group
- Journal
- Utilize digital tools and apps

Life is unpredictable, and circumstances may change along the way. That's why it's crucial to remain adaptable in your goal-setting approach. Be open to feedback, learn from setbacks, and adjust your goals to stay aligned with your evolving priorities and aspirations. Remember, it's not about rigidly adhering to a plan; it's about staying flexible and enjoying the journey.

Celebrating achievements, no matter how small, is also a vital aspect of goal-setting. Acknowledge your progress, reward yourself for your hard work, and use setbacks as opportunities for growth and learning. By cultivating a mindset of gratitude and resilience, you'll persevere through challenges and emerge stronger on the other side.

By breaking your SMART goals into manageable tasks and cultivating accountability and resilience, you'll pave the way for success and fulfillment in every area of your life. So, what are you waiting for? It's time to take the first step toward your dreams and unlock your full potential.

Enjoy the Journey
Enjoying the journey is often overshadowed by the allure of the destination. We become so fixated on reaching our objectives

that we overlook the invaluable lessons and experiences that unfold. But the truth is, the journey is an integral part of the goal-setting process — a rich time of growth, discovery, and self-mastery that shapes us into the men we are meant to be.

Cultivating the right mindset helps you to find meaning on your journey. This means you must learn how to stay fully present in each moment and savor the lessons you learn along the way. When we encounter challenges, setbacks, and triumphs that test our resolve, they help to forge our character. Allow yourself to discover your strengths, confront your weaknesses, and unearth the depths of your potential.

One of the most overlooked aspects of the journey is the opportunity for learning and growth. Approach life with curiosity and gratitude, even in the face of adversity. Every obstacle we encounter, every setback we face, is a lesson in disguise — a chance to learn, adapt, and evolve. Whether overcoming a fear, mastering a new skill, or navigating a complex problem, each challenge presents an opportunity for growth and self-improvement.

The journey is an integral part of the goal-setting process. In fact, I've learned over the years that it's equally, if not more important than achieving the goal itself. If you're open to the moments of discovery and self-mastery, you can find real growth and fulfillment. For it is in the journey that we discover our true strength and gain the potential to become the architects of our destiny.

The Bible and Goals
The Bible emphasizes the importance of planning for the future while staying humble and trusting in God. God calls us to be intentional yet flexible. He wants us to manage our resources wisely while recognizing that our ultimate dependence is on Him, not ourselves. Our goals must align with God's, and we must remain open to the possibility that God may redirect our plans for His higher purposes.

Some Christians believe that pursuing our goals goes against certain Christian beliefs and counteracts God's plan for us. On the contrary — Scriptures encourage us to pursue our goals and achieve success.

Consider these passages from the Bible:

> Jeremiah 29:11 (KJV) *"For I know the thoughts that I think toward you, saith the LORD, thoughts of peace, and not of evil, to give you an expected end."*

> Habakkuk 2:2-3 (KJV) *"And the Lord answered me, and said, Write the vision, and make it plain upon tables, that he may run that readeth it. For the vision is yet for an appointed time, but at the end it shall speak, and not lie: though it tarry, wait for it: because it will surely come, it will not tarry."*

In the book of Jeremiah, God unveils a plan crafted uniquely for you: a plan filled with wonder and greatness. It's a blueprint for triumph and happiness.

Where did God embed this plan? In your heart, undoubtedly! God has instilled within you the drive to excel and accomplish His purpose in this world. The question is, "How do I find that plan?"

Since God has placed His plan within your heart, use prayer, meditation, and wise discernment to hear His voice. Outside of prayer, be in action by asking yourself questions that may help you hear this plan more vividly.

- Identify your passion. Your deepest desires contain the seeds of God's purpose for you. Follow where your passion leads.

- Are you avoiding something? Is there something persistently gnawing at the recesses of your mind that you're attempting to evade? Your ego could be blocking God's will.
- Employ the "What, then?" technique. Ask yourself, "Once I achieve_____ _ _, what then?" Keep asking "what then" until you have this deep ah-ha experience that says, "That's it. That's the ultimate plan for my life."
- What does the Bible say about my plans? Read and pray on it, then write down or journal what bubbles up.

Most Importantly, Place Your Trust in God's Promise.

God won't unveil the entire plan all at once. After all, you might feel overwhelmed if you discover that God intended you to launch a global food enterprise, write three books annually for the next decade, or start a non-profit organization to end world hunger.

God's plan doesn't follow a linear path. It may meander, particularly when your own desires change, but God adjusts the course, ensuring you stay on track. The crux lies in trusting that God controls everything, even when your vision is limited to just a few steps ahead.

In Habakkuk 2:2-3, the prophet Habakkuk receives a powerful revelation about the significance of goal setting and the importance of aligning oneself with divine purpose. The Lord instructs Habakkuk to clearly write his vision so that others may understand and run with it. This directive underscores the importance of clarity and specificity in goal setting. By making the vision plain and tangible, it becomes something that others can grasp and pursue with determination.

The passage emphasizes the concept of divine timing; your vision may require patience and perseverance to come to fruition. It reinforces that goal setting involves making clear objectives while trusting God's timing and providence. Your vision will surely come to pass under God's plan and at the appointed time. It reminds us to align our goals with God's will and approach them with faith, patience, and perseverance.

When you align with God's plan for your life and seek His help, your goals will harmonize with His divine purpose. Your aspirations become God's aspirations for you. With His guidance, you can achieve these goals and all those that lie ahead.

Goal Summary

Setting and achieving goals is not just about reaching a destination; it's about embracing the journey and transforming our lives. In this chapter, we've delved into the essence of SMART goals — Specific, Measurable, Achievable, Relevant, and Time-bound — and discovered how they serve as the compass guiding us toward our aspirations.

But beyond the technicalities of goal-setting lies a more profound truth: the journey itself is where we find meaning, growth, and fulfillment. On this path, we encounter challenges, setbacks, and triumphs that shape us into the men we are meant to be. It's where we learn to be resilient, adaptable, and persistent in adversity. And it's where we discover our true strengths, passions, and purpose in life.

Remember to be fully present in each moment and savor the lessons life offers. We must set our sights high while remaining humble and trusting in God's purpose for us. With clarity of vision, determination, and faith, we can navigate the twists and turns of life's journey and emerge stronger, wiser, and more fulfilled on the other side.

So, let us embark on this journey of self-discovery and personal growth with courage and conviction. Let us set our goals intentionally, knowing that each step brings us closer to the life we are called to live. Trust in God's guidance and provision, knowing He has a plan and purpose for us.

With SMART goals as our compass and God as our guide, there is no limit to what we can achieve. So, let's continue on this adventure together, knowing that the best is yet to come.

Scan the code above with your smartphone
to view my chapter wrap-up video.

Go to this link to access the Chapter Worksheets:
https://truemanlifecoaching.com/TrueManTrueWaysWorksheets

Rest Stop

In the following pages, journal and reflect on your thoughts about goal setting in your journey:

_____

_____

_____

_____

_____

_____

_____

_____

_____

_____

_____

_____

_____

_____

_____

_____

_____

_____

_____

_____

_____

_____

The Horsepower of Purpose

True Man Tip

Discovering your purpose involves slowing down, calming your thoughts, and tuning into the inner voice of your heart. The heart serves as a reservoir of intelligence and wisdom, guiding you and revealing the finest aspects of your true self.

The world is full of distractions and demands, and the pursuit of purpose stands as a beacon, guiding individuals through the maze of life. Chapter Seven unveils the horsepower of purpose, which can propel you toward personal and professional fulfillment. As we examine this transformative concept, brace yourself for a journey that will redefine your understanding of passion, goals, values, and the essence of a purpose-driven life.

Creating Horsepower

In the early days of the Industrial Revolution, Scottish engineer James Watt sought a way to market and sell his steam engines. He needed a unit of measurement that could convey their power in a relatable way to potential customers. At the time, horses were commonly used to perform physical work, such as turning mill wheels or lifting loads.[25] Watt adopted the term "horsepower" as a unit of measurement to explain the rate of work his steam engines employed.

---

[25] "Horsepower." Wikipedia, June 29, 2024. https://en.wikipedia.org/wiki/Horsepower

Watt defined one horsepower as the ability to do 550 foot-pounds of work per second. This value was based on his observations of the work a horse could perform. The term "horsepower" became a widely adopted and standardized unit for expressing the power of engines and machines, and it continues to be used in this context today.

How can you create horsepower in your life to uncover your purpose?

Discovering your life's purpose requires unearthing your defining values, passions, and the ambitions that fuel you. Your true essence is forged through personal growth, relentless pursuit of your interests, and unwavering commitment to overcoming challenges.

Positively impacting the world, having meaningful connections with others, and fulfilling your career all contribute to the horsepower that propels you toward your purpose. It's a relentless journey, a direct path where resilience, determination, and a deep sense of self intertwine. Learn how to harness your horsepower, and you can learn how to shape your path and define your essence.

Lacking Purpose

When you were a young man, did you know exactly what kind of person you were meant to be? Probably not. For most of us, finding our purpose in life takes time. However, embarking on the road of life without a destination is akin to setting out on a journey without a map or compass. A driver without a destination is like a car without a navigator — aimless, wandering, and subject to the whims of the unpredictable road. Think about it this way: if you're lost in a haze of indecision, you'll struggle to find meaning in your journey.

In such a state, it's challenging to gauge progress or measure success. If you have no destination in mind, how do you know if you're moving forward? How can you celebrate reaching a milestone if you're not even sure what milestones to set?

Have you experienced this disconnect?

I'm reminded of the Biblical parable of the Prodigal Son, a timeless tale that serves as a poignant metaphor for the struggle with purpose and the subsequent journey of rediscovery.

The tale unfolds with a young man (the Prodigal Son) who comes to his father and demands his share of the inheritance. The Prodigal Son then embarks on a reckless journey. His desire for freedom and self-discovery leads him away from the sheltered walls of his father's house into a world brimming with temptations and indulgences. Initially, the newfound freedom seems exhilarating, an escape from the perceived constraints of familial obligations. The son squanders his wealth on wild living, and soon, he's left with nothing.

Can you relate to the Prodigal Son?

Then, the Prodigal Son finds himself in the midst of a famine with nothing to eat and nowhere to turn. He's adrift, disconnected from the moorings that once tethered him to meaning. The allure of fleeting pleasures becomes a mirage, and the emptiness within becomes a haunting void. It is at this juncture that the parable strikes a chord with the universal human experience — the disquieting realization of losing one's way, the erosion of purpose in the pursuit of momentary desires.

As the prodigal son grapples with the consequences of his choices, a profound transformation begins to unfold. The biblical narrative introduces a pivotal moment when the wayward son "comes to himself" in a moment of clarity. This awakening serves as a metaphorical dawn, casting light on the shadowy corners of his existence. In this introspective revelation, the prodigal son recognizes the hollowness of his pursuits and the richness of the purpose he left behind.

Returning to his father's house becomes a pilgrimage of redemption and self-discovery. Each step retraces the path of his divergence, a symbolic reconciliation with his lost purpose. The parable points to the innate human capacity for change and renewal.

It also parallels God's love and acceptance for us, which I feel ties well into the message of this chapter. Just like the father welcomed back his son, God will welcome you when you find or return to your purpose in life. The father's response to the return of his Prodigal Son adds another layer to the narrative, embodying the concept of unconditional love and forgiveness. The embrace of the father is a reminder that purpose, once lost, is not irretrievably severed.

In the modern context, the parable resonates as a timeless reflection on the human condition. The Prodigal Son's journey encapsulates the cyclic nature of purpose — its loss, discovery, and rediscovery. The tale encourages introspection, prompting individuals to pause and evaluate the trajectory of their own lives, questioning whether the pursuit of transient desires has overshadowed the enduring sense of purpose that lies within.

To avoid being or becoming another prodigal son, you must not be a blind wanderer driven solely by the adrenaline of ambition. Purpose is the North Star that guides every step, the compass that prevents a reckless drift into the abyss. Determining your purpose demands a razor-sharp clarity that cuts through the fog of uncertainty.

Understanding your purpose is not a luxury; it's a survival skill. Purpose shapes your goals, gives meaning to your actions, and strengthens your resolve in the face of adversity.

So, gentlemen, before you charge ahead, take a moment to interrogate your intentions. What fuels your dreams? What ignites the fire in your belly? Define your purpose with unyielding precision. Let your purpose navigate you like the GPS you program into your car.

Discovering Purpose

To tap into the horsepower of purpose, a man must first unearth his personal passions. Dive deep into your interests and delve into the activities that set your blood pumping with anticipation. By identifying what truly sparks your soul, you pave the way for a life filled with purpose. It's not merely about what you do; it's about what fuels your inner fire.

Let's cut to the chase. Passion isn't some abstract notion floating in space. It's the raw energy surging through you when you're immersed in something you adore. Whether it's sports, supporting a nonprofit, or strumming a guitar, pinpointing the pursuits that fill your hours with immense joy. These are the signposts directing you toward your purpose.

The crux lies not just in the action but in the sensation. Your passions serve as the breadcrumbs guiding you along the path to purpose. When you uncover what truly ignites your spirit, you're on the road to infusing purpose into every aspect of your existence.

When you take time to contemplate what genuinely sets your soul ablaze — what you'd pursue even in the absence of an audience or accolades — that, my friend, is the key to unlocking the initial gateway to a life brimming with purpose.

Discovering one's purpose in life is a deeply personal journey, and success can be defined in various ways depending on individual values and aspirations. Here are four fundamental ways for a man to explore and discover his purpose, leading to a more fulfilling and successful life:

1. Self-reflection and introspection:
    *   Take time to reflect on your values, interests, and passions. What activities make you feel most alive and engaged? Consider your strengths, weaknesses, and the things that bring you joy.
    *   Explore your past experiences and identify moments when you felt most fulfilled or accomplished. Analyze patterns and themes that emerge from these experiences.
    *   Journaling (See Chapter 2) can be a helpful tool for self-reflection. Write down your thoughts, feelings, and insights regularly to gain a deeper understanding of yourself.

2. Set meaningful goals:
    *   Establish both short-term and long-term goals that align with your values and interests. Define what success means to you, whether it's in your career, relationships, personal development, or other aspects of life.
    *   Break down your goals into actionable steps. This process can help you create a roadmap for your life and provide a sense of direction and purpose.
    *   Regularly revisit and adjust your goals as your priorities and circumstances evolve.

3. Seek new experiences:
    *   Embrace new challenges and experiences to broaden your perspective and discover hidden talents or interests. Stepping outside your comfort zone can lead to personal growth and help you uncover aspects of yourself you may not have been aware of before.

- Travel, try new hobbies, meet diverse groups of people, and engage in activities that spark curiosity. Exposure to different environments can provide valuable insights into what resonates with you on a deeper level.

4. Connect with mentors and role models:
   - Seek guidance from individuals who have achieved success in areas that align with your interests. Mentors and role models can offer valuable advice, share their experiences, and provide insights that may assist you on your journey.
   - Attend networking events, join professional or interest-based groups, join a small men's group, and build relationships with people who inspire you. Learn from their successes and challenges to gain perspective on your own path.

Remember, discovering one's purpose is an ongoing process, and it's okay for your goals and interests to evolve over time. Regularly reassessing your priorities and staying open to new opportunities will contribute to a more fulfilling and successful life.

Why Discover Purpose Matters

Without a sense of purpose, life becomes a series of tasks lacking meaning. Discovering personal passions injects vibrancy into each moment, making life a canvas for your unique expression. It's not just about finding something to do; it's about finding what makes you come alive.

In the 1993 movie "Groundhog Day," the theme of finding purpose plays a central role in transforming the lives of its characters, particularly the protagonist, Phil Connors (Bill Murray). Initially trapped in a seemingly endless loop of reliving the same day, Phil becomes disillusioned and disconnected from life. However, as he begins to recognize the futility of his actions, he embarks on a journey of self-discovery and personal growth. Phil's quest for purpose becomes a catalyst for positive change, as he starts using the repeated day to learn new skills, connect with people, and ultimately become a better version of himself.

Phil's newfound purpose also affects the lives of those around him, notably his interactions with Rita Hanson (Andie MacDowell), his co-worker and love interest. Through his evolving perspective on life, Phil learns to appreciate the value of kindness, empathy, and genuine connections with others. As he breaks free from the cycle of self-centered behavior, his relationships deepen, and he becomes a more compassionate individual. Rita, in turn, experiences a positive transformation in her own life, influenced by Phil's genuine change of heart.

The movie's exploration of purpose extends beyond individual growth to emphasize the impact on the broader community of Punxsutawney. As Phil dedicates himself to making a positive difference in the lives of others, the town undergoes a collective shift. Acts of kindness, generosity, and selflessness ripple through the community, creating a harmonious and uplifting atmosphere.

The movie Groundhog Day illustrates the profound effect of finding purpose in individual lives and the interconnectedness of personal growth with the well-being of a community. Through Phil Connors' journey, the film conveys a powerful message about the transformative power of purpose, inspiring audiences to reflect on their own lives and the impact they can have on the world around them.

Discovering one's purpose is a crucial journey for a man seeking meaning and fulfillment and avoiding the disillusionment that Phil Connors went through in the movie. Purpose serves as a guiding force, providing direction, motivation, and a sense of significance. Without a clear understanding of one's purpose, life may seem aimless and void of meaning.

Have you felt this void in your life?

Purpose gives life a sense of direction. It helps a man navigate through the challenges and opportunities that come his way. When a person is aware of their purpose, they can make choices and set goals aligned with their core values and aspirations. This sense of direction fosters a feeling of control and empowerment, allowing him to actively shape his life rather than merely reacting to circumstances.

In addition, purpose provides motivation during difficult times. Life inevitably presents obstacles, failures, and setbacks. In the face of adversity, a well-defined purpose acts as a source of resilience. It becomes the driving force propelling you forward, encouraging perseverance and a positive outlook. The awareness that one's efforts contribute to a larger, meaningful goal can transform challenges into opportunities for growth and learning.

Purpose brings a profound sense of fulfillment. If you commit to something greater than yourself, you'll experience deep satisfaction. Whether through personal relationships, professional endeavors, or community involvement, the awareness of making a meaningful impact on the world enhances the overall quality of life. This fulfillment goes beyond fleeting moments of happiness, creating a lasting and profound sense of contentment.

The journey towards a purpose-driven life requires a deliberate and introspective approach, one that demands an honest evaluation of what truly matters. It's about navigating through the maze of existence, shedding light on the dim corners of your aspirations, and discerning the sparks that ignite our souls. In a world often cluttered with distractions and obligations, it's easy to lose sight of our purpose, to drift aimlessly in the currents of routine. But by acknowledging the absence of a guiding light, we take the first step towards reclaiming control over our destinies.

Pursuing your purpose begins with an excavation of the desires and dreams that may be buried beneath layers of societal expectations and personal insecurities. It's about peeling back the layers of conditioning to uncover the raw essence of our being, to rediscover the passions that once fueled our youthful exuberance. This process demands courage and vulnerability, as we confront our fears and confront the possibility of disappointment. Yet, it's in this openness that we find our strength, for it is only by acknowledging our weaknesses that we can begin to harness our true potential.

Reflecting on my life, I realize I've always had purpose and passion, but it wasn't always well-placed or thought out. In my quest to be a True Man, I thought the shortest path was the most desirable path and the one that made the most sense. I think a lot of people feel that way. What I learned is that sometimes there is pain, loss, and sadness along the journey of understanding purpose. This cannot and should not be avoided in the belief that the shortest path wins. In fact, the true benefit is the long, hard road, which is the journey to understanding one's path.

Do you see how that could be true for you?

In essence, the journey towards a purpose-driven life is a quest for authenticity, a quest to align our actions with our values and our aspirations with our ambitions. It's about living with intention, cultivating a deep sense of gratitude for the gift of existence, and embracing the boundless possibilities that lie before us. As we embark on this journey, remember that the true measure of success lies in the lives we touch and the legacy we leave behind, for it's in the pursuit of purpose that we discover the true meaning of life itself.

Finding Purpose Through Faith
One thing is clear: we cannot navigate life's journey alone. As men, we often pride ourselves on our independence and our ability to

carve our path through the wilderness of existence. But deep down, we know there's something more, something beyond our understanding, guiding us toward our true calling.

For centuries, people have turned to faith, to the divine, to find meaning in their lives. And in this search, we discover that our purpose isn't just something we stumble upon — it's something that a higher power calls us to.

Dependence on God isn't a sign of weakness; it's recognizing our limitations as mortal beings. We are finite creatures in an infinite universe, and only by surrendering ourselves to something greater can we truly find our place in the grand scheme of things.

But how do we depend on God to help us discover our purpose in life? It begins with humility. We must set aside our desires and ambitions and listen for the still, small voice that speaks to our hearts. It requires patience; knowing that God's timing is not always our own, but trusting that He has a plan for us to give us hope and a future.

Living in a spirit-led way means allowing the Holy Spirit to guide us. It means seeking His will above our own, trusting He knows what's best for us even when we can't see the bigger picture. We must be open to His direction in every aspect of our lives.

And as we walk this path of faith, we discover our purpose unfolding before us, like a map laid out by the hands of God Himself. We may not always understand where the road leads, but we can take comfort in knowing that we are never alone and that God is always with us, guiding us every step of the way.

In his book "The Power of Significance: How Purpose Changes Your Life," John Maxwell refers to the purpose the Apostle Paul discovered while in prison.[26] The Apostle Paul expressed in Philippians 1:12-14 that the events in his life, even his imprisonment, served to advance the gospel. Maxwell highlights five ideas that Paul found, and I believe we can uncover these ourselves through a faith-filled journey toward understanding our purpose:

1. Purpose serves as a motivating force.
2. Purpose helps maintain clear priorities.
3. Purpose fosters the development of our potential.
4. Purpose empowers us to live in the present.
5. Purpose aids in evaluating our progress.

Let us embrace our reliance on God, surrender ourselves to His will, and trust that He will guide us to our calling. In Him, we discover meaning, fulfillment, and the strength and courage to fulfill our calling as men of God.

Digging Deeper into Purpose

In our current landscape, masculinity faces a crisis of identity amidst conflicting societal signals. Many grapple to understand our roles in various spheres, leading to frustration and unrealized potential. However, understanding God's purpose for them and the true nature of their relationships offers freedom and empowerment to fulfill their destiny. With this understanding, we can avoid falling into chaos, which hinders our growth and fulfillment.

The concept of purpose emerges as a central theme, emphasizing the importance of being mastered by one's purpose rather than mastering it. Purpose is a guiding force, directing individuals toward their intended destination and providing resilience against external influences. Those driven by a clear purpose are

---

[26] Maxwell, John C. The power of significance: How purpose changes your life. New York: Center Street, 2017.
https://www.amazon.com/Power-Significance-Purpose-Changes-Your/dp/1455548219

less susceptible to distraction and deviation, thus safeguarding their path to fulfillment.

Purpose is a significant aspect of salvation, constituting a substantial portion of one's spiritual journey. Unfortunately, many men languish in a state of aimlessness, resulting in a life void of an intimate relationship with Christ that could help produce the answers they seek. However, embracing Christ electrifies life with vigor and meaning, offering a pathway to salvation and fulfillment.

Scan the code above with your smartphone
to view my chapter wrap-up video.

Go to this link to access the Chapter Worksheets:
https://truemanlifecoaching.com/TrueManTrueWaysWorksheets

Rest Stop

In the following pages, journal and reflect on your thoughts about how you can achieve your purpose in life.

_____

_____

_____

_____

_____

_____

_____

_____

_____

_____

_____

_____

_____

_____

_____

_____

_____

_____

_____

_____

TRUE MAN

Chapter Eight

Navigating Vulnerability and Authenticity

True Man Tip

*Welcome the grace of God.
Present yourself to Him without limitations.
Start a path of authenticity that frees
you from hiding your true self.*

When you follow a roadmap, you had better have the right directions, and they better be clear. Life is very much the same way. If you want to get out of life what you put into it, you need to be authentic.

Have you ever felt the weight of hiding your true self? We've all been there — wearing masks to fit into societal molds, and concealing vulnerabilities out of fear. As we learned earlier, embracing vulnerability can be your greatest strength. This chapter unravels the power of authenticity and how it can transform your relationships and elevate your life.

As boys, we're taught to form an impenetrable shield around us. We have so much armor protecting ourselves that nothing will penetrate us. To show our weaknesses is like opening up a crack in the armor and exposing the heart underneath. I'm reminded of Dry Idea antiperspirant commercials from the 1980s that led with the tagline, "Never let them see you sweat."

Can you relate to that type of attitude?

Or, how about Marlon Brando's portrayal of gangster Done Vito Corleone saying, "I'm gonna make him an offer he can't refuse." Yeah, yeah, you're a real badass; I get it. Hiding behind the façade of being the tough guy is a recipe for disaster because you are not being with your true self.

Developing Your True Self

The concept of the true self for men embodies an authentic and unapologetic expression of one's core identity, values, and purpose. It involves embracing one's unique characteristics, strengths, and vulnerabilities without succumbing to societal expectations or conforming to predefined roles. To live as your authentic self requires a profound understanding of your genuine desires, passions, and beliefs and the courage to manifest them in everyday life.

Developing the true self demands a commitment to self-awareness and introspection. Men must engage in soul-searching, exploring the depths of their emotions, motivations, and aspirations. This introspective journey allows them to uncover layers of conditioning, societal pressures, and external influences that may have masked their true essence. Embracing vulnerability is a crucial aspect of this exploration, as it requires acknowledging and accepting both strengths and weaknesses.

Living in the true self necessitates breaking free from the constraints of societal expectations and traditional notions of masculinity. Men often find themselves trapped in a web of cultural stereotypes that dictate how they should behave, express emotions, or pursue success. The authentic man defies these limitations, forging his path based on his unique qualities. This may involve challenging toxic masculinity, redefining success on personal terms, and embracing a more holistic and inclusive perspective on masculinity.

On the other hand, wearing a mask or being a fraud stems from the fear of judgment, rejection, or the desire to conform to external expectations. Society often imposes rigid molds onto men, pressuring them to adopt personas that may not align with their true selves. This façade can lead to emptiness, disconnection, and inner turmoil. Shedding the mask requires a courageous act of self-discovery and a commitment to live authentically, irrespective of external opinions.

Has wearing a mask affected your relationships?

The development of the true self for men involves cultivating self-love and self-acceptance. It requires an acknowledgment that imperfections and vulnerabilities are integral parts of the human experience. Embracing these aspects empowers men to navigate life with authenticity, fostering deeper connections in relationships and a more profound sense of fulfillment. Additionally, fostering healthy relationships with others who appreciate and support their true selves is crucial for sustained growth and authenticity.

In the journey towards the true self, men should cultivate resilience and perseverance. The process involves overcoming the societal resistance, personal doubts, and discomfort that come from stepping outside predefined roles. It requires a steadfast commitment to personal growth, continuous self-reflection, and the willingness to evolve.

Ultimately, the true self for men is a dynamic and evolving concept. It is not a destination but a continuous journey of self-discovery and self-expression. To live authentically in one's true self requires the courage to embrace vulnerability, challenge societal norms, and cultivate a deep connection with one's core identity. In doing so, men can break free from the constraints of societal expectations, live with purpose, and contribute authentically to the world around them.

Addressing the Challenge of The True Self and Authenticity

In the gritty reality of our world, vulnerability is seen as a weakness, a crack in the armor that society deems unacceptable. The prevailing fear of judgment, rejection, or mockery coerces us into donning masks, shrouding our genuine selves behind a façade of stoic strength. The societal expectation to adhere to a rigid idea of masculinity further exacerbates the issue. We learn that the world values a tough exterior over authenticity and genuine connection.

However, this charade only stunts our personal evolution, strains the fabric of our relationships, and leaves us wanting. We grapple with the need to express our true selves while appearing manly and unbreakable.

Have you felt the intensity of this struggle?

But here's the kicker — the true strength lies in vulnerability. By embracing vulnerability, you open the doors to profound relationships, self-discovery, and an authentic life. It's about stripping away the layers of pretense, exposing the raw, unfiltered version of yourself that forms the bedrock of genuine connections.

Reframing our notions of masculinity requires a paradigm shift — we must put aside everything we've learned to redefine what it means to be a True Man. This is not a call to abandon strength but to change how we recognize it in ourselves and others. True power comes from navigating complex emotions, facing our fears head-on, and showing our true selves to the world. We must understand that our frailties don't make us less masculine. They make us human.

Navigating the terrain of authenticity requires resilience in the face of societal expectations. It's a rebellious act against the prescribed norms of stoicism and emotional detachment. Breaking free from the suffocating expectations the world places on us allows us to discover the liberating power of vulnerability. This isn't about baring one's soul to the world indiscriminately; it's about choosing when and where to unveil the authentic self, creating a space for genuine connections to flourish.

Creating space for vulnerability transforms relationships from superficial interactions into profound connections. Authenticity becomes a magnet that draws like-minded individuals, fostering bonds built on mutual understanding and acceptance. The richness of these connections, forged in the crucible of vulnerability, far surpasses the superficial exchanges that occur when wearing the mask of societal expectations.

In dismantling the illusion of invulnerability, you'll find a reservoir of strength that empowers you to confront challenges, cultivate meaningful relationships, and live a life that reflects the unfiltered truth of who you are. The path to authenticity is not without challenges. But, if you face them head-on, you can redefine strength on your own terms.

The Authenticity of Jesus
The most authentic man to ever walk the earth was Jesus.

Jesus serves as a quintessential model for all humanity. His unwavering commitment to truth and integrity stands as a beacon, illuminating the path for individuals seeking genuine connection and purpose. In a world often plagued by deception and duplicity, Jesus exemplified the essence of authenticity, demonstrating the profound impact of living in alignment with one's true self.

Societal expectations didn't define Jesus' life. Instead, he modeled a masculinity built on honesty, compassion, and love. His actions consistently reflected his inner convictions and principles, inspiring others to follow suit. Jesus cultivated meaningful relationships by showing others his true self and inviting them to embrace their authenticity without reservation. In a world of falsehoods and superficiality, Jesus stood as a steadfast example of integrity and truthfulness, challenging individuals to live with purpose and conviction.

Ultimately, Jesus' authenticity is a timeless reminder of the power of living in alignment with one's values and beliefs. His unwavering commitment to truth and integrity inspires people to embrace their authenticity and strive for genuine connection and meaning. As humanity navigates the complexities of existence, the example set forth by Jesus remains a guiding light, illuminating the path toward a more authentic and fulfilling existence for all.

Embracing Vulnerability as Strength
How can we embrace Jesus' authenticity and turn our weaknesses into strengths?

Jesus showed his vulnerability by expressing his emotions openly and confronting challenges honestly. He transcended the confines of societal norms, paving the way for a more profound connection with himself and those around him. Jesus' vulnerability was not a sign of fragility; it was a bridge that connected him to the hearts of those around him. Jesus's openness demonstrated inner strength — a strength emanating from an unwavering connection to his true self. By following in his footsteps, you're performing a courageous act that breaks down the walls of pretense, allowing authenticity to flourish.

Have you worn a mask or hidden from vulnerability by creating an identity that isn't your true self?

Embracing vulnerability requires deliberately confronting fear and discomfort in a whole new way. Jesus shared his deepest thoughts and emotions with his disciples, and you can, too. It's an act that fosters genuine connections, as others are invited to reciprocate and share their own vulnerabilities in a space free from judgment.

In a world that often dictates an image of unyielding masculinity, vulnerability emerges as a radical act of rebellion against the confines of stereotypes. The courage to be vulnerable allows men to shed societal expectations and embrace a truer version of themselves, much like Jesus did.

Just as Jesus faced challenges with resilience and openness, you can navigate the complexities of life with a heightened sense of self-awareness. Acknowledging your imperfections is not a sign of failure but a catalyst for learning, growth, and transformation. It paves the way for better relationships and a more fulfilling life.

As men embrace vulnerability, they not only liberate themselves from the shackles of societal expectations but also become beacons of authenticity, inspiring others to embark on their own journeys of self-discovery and genuine connection. In vulnerability, true strength is found in the example set by Jesus.

Building Authentic Connections

In the pursuit of genuine connections, authenticity reigns supreme. It's not about putting on a façade or adhering to societal expectations or the expectations you have developed over the years; it's about showing up as your true self, unapologetically and without reservation. Building authentic connections requires a willingness to be vulnerable and to share your fears, dreams, and insecurities without fear of judgment or rejection. It's in this vulnerability that true connections are forged; bonds that resonate with the essence of who you are.

One thing I strongly encourage and often recommend is building authentic connections through men's small groups. In chapter three, I shared my experience in my True Man small group. In the realm of personal growth and spiritual development, the significance of men connecting within small groups cannot be overstated.

These intimate gatherings provide a unique setting where men can come together, fostering bonds that transcend superficial interactions. Within the safe confines of such environments, individuals are encouraged to share their experiences, struggles, and triumphs openly.

This level of vulnerability cultivates a deep sense of camaraderie and mutual understanding, laying the foundation for meaningful connections. In a faith-filled environment, these connections take on added significance as they provide avenues for spiritual exploration and guidance. Through dialogue and shared reflection, men gain valuable insights into their faith, challenging and inspiring one another to delve deeper into their beliefs and values. Plus, the support and encouragement offered within these groups serve as catalysts for personal growth and transformation.

How would you like to experience this kind of relationship support?

As men navigate the complexities of life, having a supportive community to lean on can make all the difference. In men's small groups, individuals find solidarity and strength in their shared journey, empowering one another to confront challenges with courage and grace. Ultimately, the importance of men connecting within these spaces lies in the opportunity for mutual learning and growth. By coming together in a faith-filled environment, men can draw upon each other's wisdom and experiences, enriching their spiritual lives and fostering a sense of belonging that transcends individuality.

This authenticity blossoms within the nurturing confines of men's small groups, fostering an environment where men can unabashedly reveal their true selves. Here, vulnerability becomes a conduit for growth and understanding as participants courageously share their fears, aspirations, and vulnerabilities, free from the shackles of judgment or rejection. Within these sacred spaces, you can form genuine connections that resonate with the essence of each individual. Through these connections, men find solace, camaraderie, and support, cultivating a faith-filled environment where mutual learning and growth become paramount.

By embracing authenticity and vulnerability within men's small groups, men can embark on a transformative journey toward self-discovery back to their hearts. They learn from their own experiences and their fellow brothers' diverse perspectives and life journeys. In this shared exploration of faith and personal development, men can confront their innermost struggles and emerge more robust, resilient, and deeply connected to their faith and community. Thus, the importance of men connecting in small groups lies in fostering personal growth and nurturing a collective spirit grounded in authenticity, empathy, and unwavering faith.

These groups allow us to envision a world free from masks and façades, where connections in every area of your life thrive on mutual understanding and acceptance, where the essence of authenticity is paramount. Picture a scenario where men, unburdened by their masks, can foster connections that bring joy, a profound sense of belonging, and freedom to your heart.

Isn't that what you're looking for?

Building authentic connections begins with a fundamental shift in mindset — a conscious decision to embrace the vulnerability required for the deep and lasting friendships that you want. Authenticity is not a weakness; it's a declaration of strength that invites others into an arena of openness, creating a space for genuine connection.

One key aspect of forging authentic connections is the willingness to share your story. Like Jesus, whose life was an open book of teachings and experiences, men can connect on a deeper level by sharing their stories. Vulnerability becomes the bridge that spans the gap between individuals, fostering an environment where trust and understanding can flourish. By unveiling personal stories, you can inspire others to open up. This establishes a foundation of authenticity within relationships.

Listening is crucial in building authentic connections. Building genuine relationships is a two-way street; learning to listen without judgment is key. Authentic connections thrive on mutual understanding, and the art of listening allows for a more profound exchange of thoughts, emotions, and experiences. You can take this a step further by breaking free from the burden of perfectionism and learning to embrace yourself and others just as they are. When we recognize that our personal flaws add depth and richness to relationships, we can create an atmosphere where acceptance becomes the cornerstone of genuine connections.

Finally, the path to building authentic connections is paved with vulnerability and openness. It involves dismantling societal expectations and one's own life baggage, sharing personal stories, active listening, and embracing imperfections. As men embark on this path, they create a ripple effect, inspiring others to shed pretense and foster connections grounded in authenticity. The result is a world where men can thrive in relationships that resonate with their true selves, unencumbered by societal masks and enriched by the authenticity of genuine connection.

Expressing Genuine Emotions

Listen up, men. Let's get real for a moment. If you're going to have authentic relationships, you will face expressing genuine emotions. Our emotions aren't something to hide or shy away from — they make us human, but too many of us are holding back, afraid to let our true feelings show. We worry about being seen as weak or being judged. But, suppressing our emotions only holds us back from truly connecting with others and ourselves.

So, what's the solution? It's simple. We need to embrace our emotions, every single one of them. Whether joy lights up our faces, sadness weighs heavy on our hearts, or uncertainty keeps us up at night, let it out. Don't hold back. When we express ourselves authentically, we strengthen our emotional intelligence. We become more in tune with ourselves and those around us.

Sure, it's not always easy. It takes guts and courage to be vulnerable and let others see the raw, unfiltered version of ourselves. But trust me, it's worth it.

How would it feel to have deeper Connections in your life?

Let's not forget about one of the most important relationships of all — the one we have with ourselves. When we embrace our emotions, we embark on a journey of self-discovery. Each feeling becomes a guide, leading us closer to our true selves. We learn what makes us tick, what brings us joy, and what scares us. In the process, we become more alive.

It's time to stop hiding behind masks and pretending everything's okay when it's not. Let's embrace our emotions, own them, and let them guide us towards a richer life. It's time to show the world the real us — the strong, sensitive, utterly human men we are and the *True Man* we were meant to be.

Fostering Open Communication

Let's discuss a crucial aspect of building solid connections: fostering open communication. I'm talking about laying it all out there — no holding back, no beating around the bush — just straight-up, honest, transparent dialogue. Authentic relationships are the kind that last and unapologetically keep us accountable and moving in a positive direction in life.

When we can communicate openly, we're laying down sturdy bridges between us and the people we care about. Those bridges help us navigate rough patches, resolve misunderstandings, and strengthen our relationships. And let's be real here — life's too short for unnecessary drama caused by a lack of communication.

Open communication is about creating a safe space to express our deepest thoughts, fears, and dreams without fear of being judged or ridiculed. Imagine a world where we are encouraged to speak our minds and share our hearts. That's the kind of world open communication leads us to. It's a world where we can clear up misunderstandings before they fester, and resolve conflicts with empathy and understanding.

So, how do we do it? How do we become masters of open, authentic communication? Well, it starts with listening — really listening — to what others have to say. It means being honest with ourselves and with those around us. And yeah, it might take some practice, but with the right mindset and a willingness to learn, we can all become champions of open communication.

Summary of Vulnerability and Authenticity

As we wrap up this leg of our road trip, it's time to reflect on our journey. We've confronted a formidable adversary: the fear of vulnerability, a lurking shadow cast by societal narratives and learned behaviors that we've unquestioningly accepted for far too long.

We debunked false narratives by realizing that vulnerability is not a weakness but a reservoir of strength. It's the essence of our humanity, the connective tissue that binds us to others on a profound level.

Breaking free from the chains of fear is no walk in the park. It's a step-by-step process, a deliberate unraveling of the constraints that have held us captive. We started by challenging those societal narratives head-on, questioning the assumptions that have dictated our actions and limited our authenticity. By doing so, we reclaimed our right to be genuine and true to ourselves without the burden of societal judgment.

Reframing our perceptions became the cornerstone of our liberation. We no longer see vulnerability as a weakness; we recognize it as a power source. It's what makes us relatable, what makes us human.

Yet, breaking free isn't just about changing our mindset; it's about practicing self-compassion. We acknowledged that we're all works in progress, allowing ourselves the grace to stumble and fall on the path to growth. This self-compassion served as a potent weapon in dismantling the chains that bound us, reminding us that imperfection is not a flaw but a shared trait that unites us all.

We also recognized the significance of surrounding ourselves with individuals who appreciate authenticity. Building a circle that values genuine expression creates a supportive environment where everyone feels free to share their true selves. Together, we stand stronger, breaking the chains that fear once used to bind us.

Finally, we explored how Jesus embodies authenticity, leading us to true connection and purpose. His steadfast dedication to truth lights the way, revealing sincerity's strength against deceit. In a world of façades, Jesus' genuineness shines, demonstrating the profound impact of staying true to oneself. His earthly journey defines the path of the True Man. By following His example and studying the Bible's teachings, we're left with the ultimate life roadmap — an unmistakable, undeniable truth to live by.

In conclusion, we've equipped ourselves with the tools to confront and conquer the fear of authenticity and vulnerability.

It's time to step into our true power, embracing authenticity and vulnerability as the cornerstone of our strength. Let's carry this newfound understanding forward, forging a path where our true selves shine, unburdened by the chains of fear. We're men who embrace vulnerability; in doing so, we become unstoppable forces of authenticity and strength.

Scan the code above with your smartphone
to view my chapter wrap-up video.

Go to this link to access the Chapter Worksheets:
https://truemanlifecoaching.com/TrueManTrueWaysWorksheets

Rest Stop

**Journal your thoughts and think about how being
more authentic and vulnerable like Jesus can lead you
closer to becoming the True Man you want to be.**

_____

_____

_____

_____

_____

_____

_____

_____

_____

_____

_____

_____

_____

_____

_____

_____

_____

_____

_____

_____

Chapter Nine

Fueling Authentic Relationships

True Man Tip

A man's true measure starts with the preparation
of his own heart, which blossoms with authentic connections
and sincere, heartfelt love.

Picture a life where every connection you make goes beyond the surface, where every relationship you build is a source of genuine joy and support. Imagine a world where trust flows effortlessly, communication is seamless, and people coexist harmoniously. This isn't a utopian dream; it's the essence of authentic relationships, and in this chapter, we unravel the secrets to make this your reality.

Navigating the intricate paths of relationships presents challenges and complexities that test our understanding and patience. However, amidst these trials, relationships also serve as profound blessings bestowed upon us by God. They offer us opportunities for growth, connection, and love, enriching our lives in ways that often surpass our comprehension.

In this chapter, we'll address common problems like:

- Superficial connections
- Lack of meaningful relationships
- Difficulty in building trust
- Communication breakdowns

- The challenge of balancing personal and social life

The *True Man* solutions focus on prioritizing meaningful connections, building trust through authenticity, developing practical communication skills, finding the right balance between personal and social commitments, and nurturing relationships over time.

Loving Yourself

You can't examine your relationships without talking about your relationship to yourself. Hurt people, hurt people, and you don't want to be that guy. I want to get you thinking about how to heal your heart from past wounds and create a roadmap for what lies ahead.

Authentic relationships start from within. It's not some airy-fairy notion; it's a bare-knuckled reality. Before you can love someone else, you've got to confront the man staring back at you in the mirror. It's not about narcissism or self-absorption; it's about self-love, a cornerstone that lays the foundation for genuine connections.

Let's get real. Loving yourself is not some touchy-feely concept reserved for meditation gurus and poets. It's the bedrock of authentic manhood. Think about it — you can't pour from an empty cup. If a man's cup is running on fumes, what does he have to offer? A relationship built on insecurity and self-doubt is like constructing a house on shaky ground — it's destined to crumble.

It's not about being a cocky, arrogant alpha male. No, that's a thin façade that crumbles at the slightest breeze. It's about understanding your worth, acknowledging your flaws, and embracing the journey of self-improvement. Self-love is a quiet confidence, a magnetic pull that draws others in. Why? Because they can sense how grounded you are.

Are you comfortable in your own skin?

Learning to love yourself means you've done the heavy lifting of self-discovery. You've explored the crevices of your soul, faced the demons, and come out on the other side with a story to tell. It's not about perfection; it's about authenticity. Truly loving yourself means you can show the world your true self — flaws and all.

Self-love isn't about looks or wealth; it's about self-assuredness and truth. In relationships, this authenticity becomes the glue that binds two individuals. It's not a game of pretending or projecting an image to impress. Instead, it's a dance of vulnerability and mutual understanding. You can openly share your fears, dreams, and insecurities, allowing your partner to do the same.

Relationships aren't for the faint of heart. They require grit, resilience, and a deep well of self-love. When you learn to love yourself, you don't need to seek validation from outside sources. You're not on a quest to find someone to complete you, and you don't need to prove your worth to anyone.

Relationships are the vibrant threads that weave a compelling story. To create a masterpiece, a man must first master himself. It's not a solo act; it's a prelude to a symphony of shared experiences, laughter, and growth. Loving yourself requires embracing imperfections, acknowledging strengths, and nurturing self-respect.

It starts with self-awareness, understanding personal values, and setting boundaries. You must cultivate a positive mindset, celebrating achievements, big or small. Prioritize self-care, physically and mentally. Learn from failures without dwelling on them, and focus on growth. Surround yourself with supportive people. Grasp that self-love isn't selfish; it's a foundation for healthy relationships.

Accept that perfection is a myth and appreciate your unique journey. Treat yourself with the kindness you'd extend to a friend. In simplicity, self-love for a man is an ongoing, intentional practice.

Once you've mastered the genuine, God-filled love for yourself, you can embark on the journey to experience the authentic love of another. To understand how we got here, let's go back to the original biblical relationship and see how it all began.

Adam and Eve

In the Bible, the creation of Eve for Adam is depicted in the book of Genesis, symbolizing the origins of human companionship and unity. According to the story, God formed Adam from the dust of the earth and recognized that it was not good for him to be alone. In response to Adam's loneliness, God created Eve by taking a rib from Adam's side, fashioning a partner suitable for him.

The creation of Eve is significant for several reasons. It emphasizes the complementary nature of male and female, illustrating the divine intention for companionship and mutual support within the human experience. The union of Adam and Eve is portrayed as the foundation of the family unit, symbolizing the interconnectedness of humanity. Additionally, the creation of Eve underscores the idea that human relationships, particularly the marital bond, are sacred and designed by a higher power.

In addition, the narrative serves as a moral lesson, highlighting the importance of unity and cooperation. It reinforces the idea that men and women share a common origin and purpose as equal partners.

The story of Adam and Eve lays the foundation for modern-day relationships in several ways. First, it emphasizes companionship and partnership as fundamental aspects of human existence. God created Adam and Eve as equal partners that could support and complement each other. Their dynamic underscores the importance of mutual respect and cooperation in contemporary relationships.

Second, the narrative highlights the significance of trust and communication. Adam and Eve's downfall came from a break-down in trust and communication with each other and their Creator. The truth is that open and honest communication and trust are crucial for building strong bonds.

Additionally, the story underscores the concept of responsibility and accountability. Both Adam and Eve faced consequences for their actions, demonstrating that our choices carry weight and affect the individuals involved and their broader community.

Finally, Adam and Eve's story reminds us of human nature's complexities and the potential for both beauty and imperfection in relationships. It serves as a timeless Biblical story for the challenges and rewards of love, commitment, and partnership in the modern world of marriage.

Marriage and Your Commitment

Outside of your relationship with Christ, your relationship with your spouse is paramount. To be a present and loving husband and build a relationship founded on faith and love, men can draw inspiration from the story of Adam and Eve. First, it's crucial to understand the concept of companionship as demonstrated in their narrative.

It's time to recognize the importance of being present and actively engaged in your relationship. This means being emotion-ally available, listening attentively, and supporting your spouse through joys and challenges. Prioritizing your partner's well-be-ing and fostering a sense of unity can strengthen the bond with your wife.

Are you prioritizing your wife's well-being?

A strong faith helps to build a strong marital foundation. Adam and Eve's story illustrates the importance of trust in a relationship, not just between partners but also between oneself and God. Yes, Adam and Eve disobeyed God's order by bringing sin into the human race. But there is evidence that righteousness was received (Romans 5:12-21).

Couples can cultivate faith by nurturing their spiritual life individually and together. This might involve praying together, attending religious services, or engaging in meaningful discussions about faith and values. By anchoring your relationship in shared beliefs and principles, you can deepen your connection and provide a source of strength during difficult times.

Love is the cornerstone of any successful marriage. Just as Adam and Eve were meant to love and care for each other, you should prioritize consistently expressing love and affection toward your wife, including:

- verbal affirmations
- acts of kindness
- spending quality time, and
- giving thoughtful tokens of appreciation

Demonstrating your commitment and devotion can foster a sense of security and intimacy by making your partner feel cherished and valued.

You can learn from Adam's example of taking responsibility for his actions. When conflicts arise, it's essential to approach them with humility and a willingness to seek resolution. This means owning up to mistakes, apologizing sincerely, and actively working towards reconciliation. Demonstrating accountability and a desire to grow can cultivate trust and mutual respect in your marriage.

By prioritizing companionship, nurturing faith, expressing love, and taking responsibility, you can create a marriage that withstands the tests of time and strengthens your bond as a couple.

Relationships With Children

Balancing and building relationships with your children from the moment they enter this world is not just a responsibility — it's a privilege and an opportunity to shape their lives profoundly. As men, we have the power to be role models, guiding and nurturing our children as they navigate life's journey. Here's how to embark on this rewarding path and cultivate strong bonds with your kids that stand the test of time.

Be present. From the moment your child is born, show up. Be there to witness their first cries, smiles, and steps. Your presence speaks volumes, conveying love, support, and commitment. Whether changing diapers, feeding, or soothing them to sleep, every moment spent with your child is an investment in your relationship.

As your child grows, continue to be actively involved in their lives. Engage in activities that foster connection and create lasting memories. Play games together, read stories, explore nature, or simply spend quality time talking and listening. Show genuine interest in their passions and be their biggest cheerleader in their triumphs and challenges.

Communication is key. As fathers, creating an environment where your children feel comfortable expressing themselves openly and honestly is crucial. Encourage dialogue, ask questions, and actively listen to their thoughts and feelings without judgment. By fostering open communication early on, you lay the groundwork for a trusting and supportive relationship built on mutual respect.

Are you keeping the lines of communication open to your children?

Lead by example. As role models, our actions often speak louder than words. Demonstrate integrity, kindness, and empathy in your interactions with others, showing your children what it means to be a good person. Be mindful of the messages you send through your behavior, knowing that your children are watching and learning from you every step of the way.

Be involved in their education and personal development. Take an active interest in their schooling, attend parent-teacher conferences, and support their academic endeavors. Expose them to new experiences and ideas to encourage curiosity and a love of learning. Instill in them the value of perseverance and resilience, teaching them to embrace challenges as opportunities for growth.

Create traditions and rituals that strengthen your bond as a family. Whether it's a weekly movie night, a yearly camping trip, or a special birthday tradition, these shared experiences create a sense of belonging and unity. Be consistent in nurturing these traditions, reinforcing the importance of family and connection.

Finally, prioritize self-care and maintain a healthy work-life balance. As fathers, it's easy to become consumed by our professional responsibilities, but it's essential to carve out time for ourselves and our families. Remember that your well-being directly impacts your ability to be present and engaged with your children.

Building and balancing relationships with your children is a lifelong journey filled with love, joy, and growth. By being present, communicative, and leading by example, you have the power to shape their lives in profound ways. Embrace the opportunity to be a positive role model, nurturing strong bonds that will last a lifetime. Your children are counting on you, and your impact on their lives is immeasurable.

Addressing Our Relationship Challenges

Relationships constitute a crucial aspect of our lives. Upon reflection, you may observe that your happiness often corresponds with the quality of your relationships, thriving when they are strong and diminishing when they falter.

Unfortunately, when relationships falter, they can lead to negative consequences that, if left unresolved, can last a lifetime.

In his work, "The Four Things That Matter Most: A Book About Living," Dr. Ira Byock,[27] shares insights from his years in palliative care. He concluded that there are four things that matter most at the end of your life:

1. Please forgive me.
2. I forgive you.
3. Thank you.
4. I love you.

Navigating the complexities of relationships requires courage and commitment. It demands an acknowledgment of our vulnerabilities and a willingness to communicate openly and honestly. Often, our pride stands in the way, preventing us from extending forgiveness or expressing gratitude. Yet, as Dr. Byock emphasizes, these four simple yet profound phrases hold the power to mend even the most broken relationships.

In our quest for relationship fulfillment, we must prioritize cultivating genuine connections over the superficial interactions that could lead to regret, shame, and sorrow. It's about quality

---

[27] Byock, Ira. The four things that matter most: Essential wisdom for transforming your relationships and your life. New York: Free Press, 2004.

over quantity, depth over breadth. Taking the time to truly listen, understand, and empathize with our loved ones can transform shallow relationships into meaningful bonds that withstand the test of time.

Are you taking the time to truly listen, understand, and empathize with your loved ones?

Building and maintaining healthy relationships has its challenges. Misunderstandings, conflicts, and differing perspectives are inevitable. Yet, how we choose to navigate these obstacles ultimately defines the strength of our relationships. Instead of avoiding discomfort, we must confront issues head-on, seeking resolution through empathy, compromise, and mutual respect.

It's essential to prioritize self-awareness and personal growth within our relationships. Recognizing our flaws and actively working to improve ourselves not only benefits us individually but also strengthens our connections with others. By continuously striving to be better partners, friends, and family members, we create a positive ripple effect that enriches our lives.

In essence, addressing our relationship challenges requires a concerted effort from all parties involved. It demands vulnerability, empathy, and a genuine commitment to fostering meaningful connections. By embracing Dr. Byock's four essential phrases and prioritizing authentic human interactions, we can cultivate relationships that bring us true happiness and fulfillment by prioritizing them.

Prioritizing Meaningful Connections

Authenticity reigns supreme in the realm of meaningful connections. The fact is, all of this goes together if you want to have loving relationships. Guess what? The door swings both ways as well!

Authenticity is about having the right people around you. It involves being true to yourself and expecting the same from those in your inner circle.

Imagine your relationships as a mirror reflecting your true self. When you prioritize authenticity, that reflection becomes crystal clear. It means showing up as you are, flaws and all, and encouraging others to do the same. In a world often dominated by masks and pretenses, embracing authenticity becomes a powerful act of rebellion.

Authentic connections transcend the surface, delving into the depths of shared values, interests, and vulnerabilities. To create a safe space for growth and self-discovery, surround yourself with people who appreciate the real you. Authenticity builds trust, fostering an environment where you can express your thoughts and feelings without fear of judgment.

So, how do you cultivate authenticity in your relationships?

Start by being honest about your own experiences, thoughts, and emotions. Share your successes and failures, your dreams and fears. Encourage open communication within your circle, creating a culture of transparency and vulnerability. This deepens your connections and sets the stage for others to reciprocate, strengthening the bonds that tie your social garden together.

Effective Communication
In the intricate dance of relationships, communication is the music that guides your steps. Effective communication involves more than just words; it's about truly understanding and being understood. It's an art that requires practice, patience, and a genuine desire to connect.

Consider communication as a bridge between minds. To strengthen that bridge, you must be intentional in your efforts. Actively listen to others, seeking to comprehend the words they speak and the emotions behind them. Practice empathy, putting yourself in their shoes to grasp their perspective fully.

Express yourself clearly and assertively. Be open about your needs, desires, and boundaries. Effective communication involves talking and listening, creating a balanced exchange that fosters mutual understanding.

Do you listen or talk more?

Unresolved issues in relationships often stem from miscommunication. By honing your communication skills, you dismantle barriers and pave the way for genuine connection. It's not about being a master orator but a thoughtful communicator who values exchanging ideas and emotions.

Prioritizing meaningful connections, embracing authenticity, and mastering effective communication lay the foundation for fulfilling and lasting relationships. As we navigate the intricacies of human connection, these elements serve as the keys to unlocking the profound joy, support, and growth that authentic relationships can bring to our lives. Tend to your social garden carefully, be true to yourself and those around you, and dance through life with the harmonious rhythm of effective communication.

Building Trust
Building trust through authenticity is akin to constructing a solid foundation for a lasting structure. In relationships, trust is the framework that supports openness, vulnerability, and genuine connection. In this context, authenticity is the raw material that binds these elements together, creating a structure built to withstand the tests of time.

Consider the analogy of a building. Trust is the foundation upon which everything rests. It provides stability, allowing the structure to rise confidently. On the other hand, authenticity is the substance within the walls — the bricks that form the structure's core. When you are genuine, you become a trustworthy individual, someone others can rely on because they know who you truly are.

Authenticity involves peeling away the layers of pretense and embracing vulnerability. It's about showing your true self, even if that means revealing imperfections. When you share your successes, failures, dreams, and fears, you lay the groundwork for trust to flourish. Others perceive your authenticity as a signal that you can be trusted, fostering a sense of security within the relationship.

Do people trust being in relationships with you?

Trust is the currency that facilitates open communication. When trust is present, individuals feel safe expressing their thoughts and emotions without the fear of judgment. This, in turn, cultivates an environment conducive to collaboration, problem-solving, and mutual support.

Think about a team working together on a project. Trust is the glue that binds them, enabling effective communication and cooperation. Authenticity plays a pivotal role in this dynamic. When team members are authentic about their strengths and weaknesses, ideas flow freely, and innovation thrives. It's a shared understanding that everyone is bringing their genuine selves to the table, fostering a sense of camaraderie and collective achievement.

Authenticity builds a bridge between hearts in personal relationships, whether with friends, family, or a romantic partner. It allows for sharing intimate thoughts and feelings, creating a deep sense of connection. When both parties are authentic, the relationship becomes a safe haven where trust flourishes, providing the emotional support needed to weather life's storms.

To build trust through authenticity, be honest with yourself and others. Acknowledge your strengths and weaknesses, successes and failures. Communicate openly and transparently, setting the stage for reciprocal honesty. Remember, authenticity is not about presenting a polished façade but about being genuine and honest.

Balancing Social and Personal Commitments

Balancing our personal and social commitments can be a pivotal challenge. Finding equilibrium requires deliberate intentionality amid career, family, friendships, and self-care demands. Visualize your time and energy as precious commodities, finite and in constant demand. By conscientiously distributing these resources, you safeguard against the pitfalls of neglecting either personal pursuits or social connections. Establishing clear boundaries becomes imperative, empowering you to assertively decline obligations that encroach upon your well-being while prioritizing activities that enrich your life.

Why does achieving this balance matter? The repercussions of an imbalance reverberate across all facets of our existence, manifesting as burnout, strained relationships, and a pervasive sense of disillusionment. Neglecting personal endeavors may lead to a loss of identity and fulfillment, while forsaking social connections can cause feelings of isolation and detachment. Striking a balance ensures you can navigate life's intricacies with resilience and authenticity.

Imagine a tightrope walker gracefully traversing the tight line between two towering skyscrapers. Each step requires unwavering focus and equilibrium. Similarly, mindfulness is paramount in the balancing act of personal and social commitments. It entails constantly recalibrating priorities, an unwavering commitment to self-care, and a willingness to adapt as circumstances evolve.

Central to this equilibrium is the cultivation of self-awareness. Take stock of your values, aspirations, and boundaries. Understand your limits and honor your needs without guilt or apology. Embrace the power of saying no. Recognize that declining invitations or opportunities is a testament to your commitment to self-preservation.

At the same time, cherish and nurture your social connections. Invest in meaningful relationships that bring joy, support, and growth into your life. Carve out dedicated time for shared experiences, whether intimate gatherings with loved ones or engaging in community activities that align with your interests and values.

Achieving a balance between personal and social commitments is a dynamic and ongoing process. It requires patience, self-reflection, and prioritizing one's well-being amidst life's myriad distractions. By embracing this equilibrium, one forges a life rich in fulfillment, authenticity, and connection.

Nurturing Relationships Over Time

Nurturing relationships over time is like tending to a garden: it requires dedication, patience, and a willingness to adapt to changing seasons. The most profound relationships are formed through a series of shared experiences, conversations, and gestures of care. It's about showing up consistently, even when life throws curveballs, and demonstrating unwavering support and commitment to each other's well-being.

The essence of nurturing relationships lies in the simple yet profound act of being present. Whether through regular check-ins, quality time spent together, or heartfelt conversations, showing up for the people who matter most is essential. It's about being there to listen, to lend a helping hand, or simply to share a laugh during the highs and offer a shoulder to lean on during the lows.

Why does this ongoing investment matter? Because lasting relationships serve as pillars of strength amid life's uncertainties. They provide a sense of stability, belonging, and security that enrich our lives in tangible and intangible ways. Whether it's a lifelong friendship, a romantic partnership, or a bond with family members, these connections form the fabric of our support system, helping us navigate the ups and downs of life with resilience and grace.

Nurturing relationships over time fosters a sense of shared memories and mutual understanding. As we journey through life together, we accumulate memories, overcome challenges, and celebrate milestones, all of which contribute to the depth and richness of our connections. These shared experiences create countless stories and moments that bind us, reinforcing the bonds of camaraderie, trust, and love.

In essence, nurturing relationships over time is a labor of love — an ongoing commitment to cultivating meaningful connections that stand the test of time. It's about recognizing the value of investing in the people who enrich our lives and dedicating ourselves to fostering growth, respect, and reciprocity in our relationships.

Chapter Summary

As we conclude this chapter and this leg of our road trip, it's crucial to emphasize the significance of prioritizing your own life. Shifting blame onto others for your situation and evading responsibility for your life is not conducive to a fulfilling existence or building relationships. While unforeseen events may occur or may have occurred in your life, they present opportunities for growth, healing, and redemption.

The Bible provides two scriptures that I believe are highly important to end on as they relate to relationships:

"A new commandment I give unto you, That ye love one another; as I have loved you, that ye also love one another. By this shall all men know that ye are my disciples, if ye have love one to another."
John 13:34-35 KJV

"Therefore, all things whatsoever ye would that men should do to you, do ye even so to them: for this is the law and the prophets."
Matthew 7:12

When it comes to your relationship, always ask yourself these two questions:

- Is this how I would like to be treated?
- What would Jesus do?

Scan the code above with your smartphone
to view my chapter wrap-up video.

Go to this link to access the Chapter Worksheets:
https://truemanlifecoaching.com/TrueManTrueWaysWorksheets

Rest Stop

Journal and reflect on your thoughts concerning relationships and contemplate ways to cultivate stronger connections in your life, guiding you towards becoming the True Man you want to be.

_____

_____

_____

_____

_____

_____

_____

_____

_____

_____

_____

_____

_____

_____

_____

_____

_____

_____

Chapter Ten

Revving up Physical Vitality

True Man Tip

Maintaining an active lifestyle and consuming nutritious foods can elevate your daily performance, uplift your mood, enhance focus, and promote better sleep. Our bodies excel when engaged in movement. They operate more efficiently when we prioritize healthy dietary choices and a regular dietary regimen.

From a young age, I've always been active — whether it was running, playing sports, or even a quick game of kick-the-can, physical activity was a constant in my life. Movement and being in action are all I've ever known.

As we age, life gets busier, and with the natural decline in hormone levels and metabolism, there's a risk of not aging as gracefully as we might hope. As I've aged I started to notice a creeping lack of energy and vitality that I wasn't prepared for.

Although I never saw myself as obese, my doctor's Body Mass Index (BMI) calculator suggested otherwise. While I don't fully agree with how BMI is calculated, the undeniable truth was that I wanted to be healthier and have more energy.

I found a doctor who could help me achieve my weight and health goals. Without diving into all the details, I encourage you to find a doctor who's willing to work with you to help you reach your goals. As I write this, I've successfully lost and kept off 25 pounds.

What has this done for me? I'm sleeping better, my heart rate has improved, my energy levels have increased, and overall, I feel exceptional. These benefits are also available to you. I highly encourage you to take action to improve your health and enjoy a more active life.

Why is this important?

A lack of physical activity leads to:

- An increased risk of chronic diseases like type 2 diabetes, heart disease, and certain types of cancers[28]
- A sedentary lifestyle is associated with Osteoporosis, chronic pain, musculoskeletal diseases, and premature death[29]
- An increase in stress levels, which may cause tension, irritability, and mental exhaustion
- Feelings of inadequacy, low self-esteem, diminished self-confidence, and dissatisfaction, and
- An endless cycle of avoiding exercise, which further exacerbates mental health issues and perpetuates the cycle of inactivity

According to the Journal of American Medical Association, 72% of American men are overweight or obese versus 64% of

---

[28] "Risks of Physical Inactivity." Johns Hopkins Medicine, March 4, 2024. https://www.hopkinsmedicine.org/health/conditions-and-diseases/risks-of-physical-inactivity.

[29] Park, Jung Ha et al. "Sedentary Lifestyle: Overview of Updated Evidence of Potential Health Risks." *Korean journal of family medicine* vol. 41,6 (2020): 365-373. doi:10.4082/kjfm.20.0165

women.[30] In an article entitled, The Obesity Epidemic: It's a Guy Thing, Dr. John La Puma said, "There's a lot more illness among men, and a lot less healthcare... Men are asleep at the wheel of their health."[31]

Men, what happens when we fall asleep at the wheel? The consequences could make you sick or worse. If you're going to be the best True Man you can be, you must take control of your health.

This chapter empowers you to take charge of your physical health and vitality through practical guidance and evidence-based research. By incorporating regular exercise, adopting healthy nutrition habits, prioritizing adequate sleep and recovery, and understanding the mental health benefits of physical activity, you can start movement toward revitalizing your physical vitality. By revving up physical vitality, men can unlock a newfound energy, and resilience that enhances every aspect of their lives.

Sedentary lifestyle

A sedentary lifestyle, characterized by prolonged periods of sitting or low levels of physical activity, poses significant health risks for men. This lifestyle has become increasingly common, driven by desk jobs, passive entertainment options, and reliance on technology. While it may seem harmless to spend long hours sitting, the consequences can harm physical and mental health.

An inactive lifestyle can contribute to weight gain and obesity, which further exacerbates other health problems. It can also lead

---

[30] Flegal, Katherine M. "Prevalence and Trends in Obesity among US Adults, 1999-2008." *JAMA* 303, no. 3 (January 20, 2010): 235–41. https://doi.org/10.1001/jama.2009.2014.

[31] Goldman, Erik. "The Obesity Epidemic: It's a Guy Thing." Holistic Primary Care, October 30, 2013. https://holisticprimarycare.net/topics/chronic-disease/the-obesity-epidemic-its-a-guy-thing-2/.

to muscle weakness, joint stiffness, and poor posture, contributing to chronic pain and mobility issues.

Have you experienced these types of issues?

Furthermore, a sedentary lifestyle is associated with adverse effects on mental health. Research has found a correlation between sedentary behavior and increased risk of depression, anxiety, and other mental health disorders.[32] Lack of physical activity can lead to decreased endorphins and serotonin (neurotransmitters that play a role in mood regulation).

Another problem with a sedentary lifestyle is its impact on overall quality of life. Men who lead sedentary lives often report lower levels of energy, vitality, and overall well-being compared to those who are more physically active. Sedentary individuals may also experience social isolation and decreased social engagement, as they are less likely to participate in physical activities or social events that involve movement.[33]

Addressing this problem requires consciously reducing prolonged periods of sitting and incorporating more physical activity into daily life, such as regular exercise and active leisure activities. If you feel overwhelmed, just remember to start small. You will see health benefits by just incorporating 20 minutes of moderate physical activity each day.[34]

---

[32] Ellingson, Laura D et al. "Changes in sedentary time are associated with changes in mental wellbeing over 1 year in young adults." *Preventive medicine reports* vol. 11 274-281. 30 Jul. 2018, doi:10.1016/j.pmedr.2018.07.013

[33] Wu, Xiu Yun et al. "The influence of physical activity, sedentary behavior on health-related quality of life among the general population of children and adolescents: A systematic review." *PloS one* vol. 12,11 e0187668. 9 Nov. 2017, doi:10.1371/journal.pone.0187668

[34] Park, Jung Ha et al. "Sedentary Lifestyle: Overview of Updated Evidence of Potential Health Risks." *Korean journal of family medicine* vol. 41,6 (2020): 365-373. doi:10.4082/kjfm.20.0165

Slowly increase this amount over time for even more benefits.

Tips for incorporating physical activity at an office job:

- Join a lunchtime walking or running group. No group available? Set one up!
- Depending on your office or home facilities, you might have access to a gym or fitness room to do yoga, swim, or gym workouts. You can do these before work, after work, or during your lunch break.
- Ask your boss if you can get a standing desk. And plan standing or walking meetings.
- Meet outside so you can walk while you talk.
- Take regular breaks from your computer. Every 30 minutes, stand up and move around.
- Walk somewhere for lunch, preferably outside.
- Rotate sitting tasks (such as emails) with standing tasks (such as photocopying or presentations).
- Use the stairs instead of the elevator.
- Drink more water. Going to the water cooler and bathroom will break up your sitting time.[35]

Breaking free from sedentary habits and prioritizing physical activity can improve your health, vitality, and well-being.

Are you neglecting physical fitness and mental fitness?

Lack of Physical Fitness and Mental Health Problems

The mental health impacts of physical inactivity represent a significant problem for many men, often leading to a range of psychological and emotional challenges. Despite the well-documented benefits of exercise for mental health, many men

[35] Department of Health & Human Services. "Physical Activity - How to Get Active When You Are Busy." Better Health Channel, January 10, 2017. https://www.betterhealth.vic.gov.au/health/healthyliving/Physical-activity-how-to-get-active-when-you-are-busy.

lead sedentary lifestyles, which can exacerbate existing mental health issues or contribute to the development of new ones.

One of the primary problems associated with physical inactivity is the increased risk of depression and anxiety. Research has consistently shown that regular exercise can help alleviate symptoms of depression and anxiety by stimulating the release of endorphins, neurotransmitters that promote feelings of happiness and relaxation.

Regular exercise:

- Improves mental clarity, cognitive function, memory, and concentration
- Reduces risk of cognitive decline and dementia
- It is a powerful stress reliever, helping to reduce levels of cortisol (the body's primary stress hormone), and
- Enhances body image, self-esteem, and overall self-perception.

Have you experienced this?

Addressing this issue requires promoting awareness of the mental health benefits of exercise and providing support and resources to help individuals incorporate regular physical activity into their daily lives. By prioritizing physical activity, men can improve their mental well-being, enhance their overall quality of life, and reduce their risk of mental health disorders.

Exercise has numerous benefits for mental health, including reducing symptoms of depression, anxiety, and stress. Physical activity stimulates the release of endorphins, neurotransmitters that promote happiness and relaxation, improving mood and overall well-being. When men neglect physical fitness, they miss out on these mental health benefits, leaving them vulnerable to the harmful effects of stress and mental illness.

Easy Movement and Exercise Tips for Your Daily Life

- While waiting in line, balance on one foot for a few seconds, then the other. Gradually build up the length of time you can balance.
- At your desk, stand up and do a few leg raises or toe stands to strengthen your legs.
- While waiting for your morning coffee, do a few wall push-ups or calf stretches.
- When you brush your teeth, do 10 squats.
- While watching television, do stretches and core exercises or pedal a stationary bike. Or maybe try to do 20 star jumps and 20 couch push-ups.[36]

Poor health habits

Poor health habits represent a significant challenge for many men, often leading to a variety of health issues and diminished overall well-being. These habits encompass a range of behaviors, such as:

- excessive consumption of ultra-processed foods, sugary beverages, and fast food
- inadequate nutrition
- smoking
- substance use issues, such as excessive alcohol consumption, and
- irregular sleep patterns

We all know we should eat healthier but cooking and planning take time and effort. Sometimes, take-out seems like the simplest and most convenient choice. But those drive-thru trips might cost you more than you think. Did you know that consum-

---

[36] List comes from "Department of Health & Human Services. Physical Activity - How to Get Active When You Are Busy." Better Health Channel, January 10, 2017. https://www.betterhealth.vic.gov.au/health/healthyliving/Physical-activity-how-to-get-active-when-you-are-busy.

ing high amounts of ultra-processed foods, sugary beverages, and saturated fats can lead to conditions like obesity, type 2 diabetes, and cardiovascular disease?[37]

Unhealthy lifestyle choices can also lead to feelings of lethargy, low energy, and mood disturbances, affecting overall quality of life and psychological functioning.[38] For example, excessive alcohol consumption may initially provide temporary relief from stress or anxiety but can ultimately exacerbate mental health issues and lead to dependency or addiction. Similarly, inadequate sleep patterns can impair cognitive function, mood regulation, and mental health.

To address this issue, we need to gather information to make good choices and attain resources to help adopt healthier lifestyle choices. By positively changing your health habits, you can improve your quality of life, reduce your risk of chronic disease, and enhance your overall well-being.

Difficulty in Establishing a Fitness Routine

If this sounds familiar, you are not alone. Many of us need help establishing a consistent fitness routine. Even when we want to exercise, we cannot form a consistent routine due to various factors such as busy schedules, demanding work commitments, and family responsibilities. Many men find it challenging to carve out dedicated time for physical activity amidst competing priorities, leading to inconsistent or sporadic exercise habits.

---

[37] LaMotte, Sandee. "Ultraprocessed Foods Linked to Heart Disease, Diabetes, Mental Disorders and Early Death, Study Finds." *CNN*. February 28, 2024. https://www.cnn.com/2024/02/28/health/ultraprocessed-food-health-risks-study-wellness/index.html#:~:text=%E2%80%9CUltraprocessed%20foods%20are%20high%20in,type%202%20diabetes%20and%20hypertension.%E2%80%9D.

[38] Lachance, Laura, and Drew Ramsey. "Food, mood, and brain health: implications for the modern clinician." *Missouri medicine* vol. 112,2 (2015): 111-5.

How are you prioritizing your time to include a healthy fitness routine?

Have you ever wanted to go to the gym regularly but stopped because you didn't know where to start? Even getting started seems daunting or overwhelming for those with limited physical activity experience. Uncertainty about which exercises to perform, how to use gym equipment, or how to create a balanced workout plan can create barriers to getting started.

Other challenges:

- Lack of motivation or accountability
- No access to a gym or fitness center
- Financial constraints or limited access to transportation
- Setbacks like injuries or illnesses

When faced with setbacks, you may feel discouraged and need help maintaining motivation in your exercise regimen. After all, it's hard to stay consistent without external support or encouragement. Additionally, self-doubt or insecurity can further erode motivation, making it difficult to sustain long-term habits.

Your Body is a Temple

Before discussing solutions for revving physical vitality, let's examine how the Bible views your body. In 1 Corinthians 6:19–20, the Apostle Paul states plainly: "Your body is a temple of the Holy Spirit within you... so glorify God in your body." This verse underscores two fundamental truths.

First, your primary purpose is to bring glory to your Creator. Second, the care you give to your body is an outward expression of honoring God. It's an essential aspect of responsibly managing the gifts entrusted to you during your time on earth —a concept Jesus frequently emphasized through his teachings.

1 Corinthians 6:19 serves as a potent reminder of the sanctity of our bodies, designated as temples housing the Holy Spirit. It urges us to cherish and maintain our physical, mental, and emotional well-being, aligning our lives with God's principles. This verse also underscores the impact on our relationships, choices, and conduct. As followers of Christ, we must acknowledge that our bodies aren't ours alone; they're consecrated for divine objectives.

I personally haven't always done a great job taking care of myself. It's easy to get lazy and submit to excuses. However, when you think of your body as divinely created by God and something you should take sacred care of, you begin to look at health through a different lens.

God wants you to be healthy. My hopes and prayers for you echo Paul's sentiments to the Thessalonian congregation. And the very God of peace sanctify you wholly; and I pray God your whole spirit and soul and body be preserved blameless unto the coming of our Lord Jesus Christ. (1 Thessalonians 5:23 KJV)

Addressing this issue requires recognizing and overcoming barriers to exercise, finding strategies to stay motivated and accountable, and seeking support and guidance to establish sustainable habits. By prioritizing consistency and perseverance, men can overcome challenges and establish a fitness routine that supports their health and well-being in the long term.

A Roadmap to Creating a Sustainable Fitness Routine

The first step in prioritizing your health is incorporating regular exercise into your daily or weekly schedule. But let's face it, establishing a routine can be a real challenge, so here are some quick ideas to get you going:

- **Set goals that are clear and attainable:**
  Begin with SMART goals that are specific, measurable, and realistic to help you stay motivated and on track. To keep track of progress and keep going, break down bigger goals into smaller, more doable steps. Make sure to celebrate your progress.

- **Identify and Address Barriers:**
  Take time to identify what is stopping you from exercising, like not having enough time, energy, or confidence. Come up with ways to overcome these problems, such as changing your schedule, starting with shorter workouts, or gradually increasing intensity.

- **Set a routine and stick to it**:
  Being consistent is important for making habits that last. Set aside the same time every day or week to work out. It can help you find activities you enjoy and are likely to stick with long-term, whether that's walking, jogging, cycling, swimming, or participating in group fitness classes.

- **Mix Up Your Workouts:**
  To avoid getting bored or burned out, change your workout schedule. To keep things interesting and work out a lot of different muscle groups, mix up your workouts by doing things like running, strength training, flexibility exercises, and activities outside. Aim for at least 150 minutes of moderate-intensity aerobic activity per week.

- **Find a Workout Buddy or Community**:
  Join a fitness class or look for a workout partner to get support. Find a friend to meet up with at the gym weekly or join a group activity like bowling, basketball, or golf. This will provide accountability, socialization, and fun.

If you prioritize exercise, you can build strength, improve cardiovascular health, and boost your overall well-being. By creating sustainable fitness routines, you can establish lifelong habits supporting your health and well-being for years.

Nutrition and Sleep

Another essential aspect of health is adopting wholesome nutrition habits to fuel your body properly. Focus on consuming a balanced diet rich in fruits, vegetables, whole grains, lean proteins, and healthy fats. Prioritize nutrient-dense foods that provide sustained energy and support muscle recovery and growth. Additionally, staying hydrated by drinking plenty of water throughout the day is crucial for optimal performance and overall health.

Sleep is crucial to health and well-being. Aim for 7-9 hours of quality sleep daily to support muscle repair, hormone regulation, and cognitive function.[39] Establish a regular sleep schedule and create a relaxing bedtime routine to promote restful sleep. I know this will be hard, but put your phone away 2 hours before bed to help you fall asleep faster. The blue light from your phone impacts REM cycles and sleep quality.[40]

Additionally, incorporate rest days into your exercise routine to allow your body time to recover and prevent overtraining. Engage in relaxation and stress reduction activities, such as yoga, meditation, or deep breathing exercises. Prioritizing sleep and recovery will enhance your physical performance, reduce the risk of injury, and support overall health and well-being.

---

[39] Medical News Today. "Why Is Sleep Important? 9 Reasons for Getting a Good Night's Rest." Medical News Today. Accessed August 11, 2024. https://www.medicalnewstoday.com/articles/325353.

[40] Rafique, Nazish et al. "Effects of Mobile Use on Subjective Sleep Quality." *Nature and science of sleep* vol. 12 357-364. 23 Jun. 2020, doi:10.2147/NSS.S253375

Final Thoughts on Physical Vitality

This chapter underscores the crucial link between physical activity and mental well-being, emphasizing the importance of prioritizing physical health for optimal outcomes. Exercise profoundly influences mood, stress levels, self-esteem, cognitive function, and susceptibility to mental health disorders.

Understanding these effects empowers individuals to proactively integrate regular physical activity into their routines.

Physical and mental fitness requires overcoming common obstacles and establishing sustainable habits. It starts with making exercise a daily priority. Setting achievable goals, staying motivated, and seeking support from peers, family, or fitness professionals facilitate adherence to an exercise regimen.

Eating a nutritious diet and prioritizing sufficient sleep and recovery are integral components of fitness maintenance. Nourishing the body with wholesome foods, getting adequate rest, and appreciating the positive impact of exercise on mental well-being optimize overall health outcomes.

In addition, faith should play a significant role in how you treat your body and think about yourself. Your body is a temple that should glorify God.

By adopting healthy lifestyle practices and seeking assistance, when necessary, men can embark on a journey toward improved fitness and enhanced well-being. Through dedication, consistency, and a commitment to self-care, men can unleash the transformative potential of physical activity and reap its manifold benefits in the long term.

Scan the code above with your smartphone
to view my chapter wrap-up video.
Go to this link to access the Chapter Worksheets:
https://truemanlifecoaching.com/TrueManTrueWaysWorksheets

Rest Stop

Journal and reflect on your thoughts on physical vitality and how you begin to improve your health and work on becoming the True Man you want to be.

_____

_____

_____

_____

_____

_____

_____

_____

_____

_____

_____

_____

_____

_____

_____

_____

_____

_____

_____

_____

Chapter Eleven

Road Less Traveled to Financial Empowerment

True Man Tip

One of life's greatest hurdles is remaining true to oneself without conforming to the riches the rest of the world claims to have. Don't keep up with your neighbors. Stay true to yourself.

If you believe what you see online and on social media, you may be tempted to think everyone has a private aircraft and drives a Rolls-Royce. However, on the road trip through this book, you will discover that this is simply not the case.

There is a major temptation in this world to finance everything and live beyond our means to support an identity that does not exist (see Chapter One). Ask yourself if this is about prioritizing your family and yourself, or is this all about keeping up with your neighbors? The temptation is real, but to become the True Man you were meant to be, you may have to take the road less traveled and learn how to live within your means for the glory of God.

Financial empowerment plays a pivotal role in the pursuit of a fulfilling and successful life, providing individuals with the means to achieve their goals, support their families, and secure their future. For men, navigating the world of personal finance can often feel like traversing an unfamiliar road, fraught with challenges and uncertainties. However, by embracing a proactive approach to financial empowerment and seeking guidance on the less traveled paths to financial success, men can pave the way toward greater stability, security, and prosperity.

This chapter looks into the unique challenges and opportunities men encounter on their journey towards financial well-being. From overcoming financial instability and debt to pursuing fulfilling career paths and planning for the future, this chapter explores the multifaceted aspects of financial empowerment and provides practical insights and strategies for achieving financial success.

In today's rapidly evolving economic landscape, financial literacy and empowerment have become more important than ever. However, many men face obstacles such as lack of financial education, debt accumulation, and uncertainty about their financial future. By addressing these challenges head-on and embracing alternative approaches to financial management, men can unlock new possibilities and pave their own paths to prosperity.

Through education and tools, you can empower yourself to take control of your financial destiny, which will allow you to achieve greater financial stability, independence, and freedom. Throughout this chapter, we will explore the importance of:

- financial education
- budgeting
- debt management
- career planning
- and long-term financial planning

By embracing proactive financial management strategies and exploring alternative paths to success, you can overcome challenges, seize opportunities, and achieve lasting financial empowerment.

Financial Challenges

Financial instability poses a significant challenge for many men and their families, affecting their ability to achieve financial security and pursue their goals. Many of us face uncertain employment status, with jobs susceptible to layoffs, downsizing, wage cuts, or outsourcing. Additionally, economic fluctuations can lead to periods of unemployment or underemployment, making it difficult for many people to maintain consistent income streams to support themselves and their families.

Also, working-age men are dropping out of the labor force. According to the Bureau of Labor Statistics, only 89 percent of working-age men have a job or are actively looking for work. In 1950, that number was at 97 percent.[41] Unemployment, underemployment, and falling wages are especially problematic for non-college-educated men. According to Fortune magazine, their pay has shrunk by more than 30% since 1980 compared to the average earnings of all other prime-age workers. Their weekly earnings have declined by 17%, while those of college-educated men rose by 20%.[42] Major cuts in middle-class manufacturing jobs and wage inequality have impacted many men's income and quality of life.

Overspending and accumulating debt can also lead to economic instability. Without proper budgeting and financial planning, you may struggle to provide for your family and meet your finan-

---

[41] Blake, Suzanne. "Rising Number of Men Don't Want to Work." *Newsweek*. May 6, 2024. https://www.newsweek.com/american-men-dont-want-work-anymore-1897567.

[42] Prakash, Prarthana. "Men Are Dropping out of the Labor Force Because They're Upset about Their Social Status, According to a New Study." *Fortune*. Fortune, December 7, 2022. https://fortune.com/2022/12/07/men-dropping-out-work-force-status-study/amp/.

cial obligations, leading to stress, anxiety, and a difficult-to-break cycle of debt. Additionally, unexpected life events such as medical emergencies, accidents, or natural disasters can lead to bankruptcy and other problems. Without adequate savings or insurance coverage, men may face significant financial hardships when faced with unforeseen expenses, leading to further strain on their finances and overall well-being.

Financial instability can have far-reaching consequences beyond the individual level, impacting families, communities, and society. Due to financial struggles, families may experience increased stress and tension, leading to marital discord, family breakdown, and negative outcomes for children. As for the larger social impact, when industries or companies move out of cities and neighborhoods, it can devastate the people who live there, leaving the community to suffer from decreased economic activity and social cohesion.

Have you experienced this?

When this occurs communities bear the burden of increased reliance on social welfare programs and support services to assist those facing financial hardship.

Addressing this issue requires a multifaceted approach, including policies to improve economic stability (such as education, apprenticeships, and job training programs) and providing support and resources to those facing financial challenges. By addressing the root causes of economic instability and implementing practical solutions, we can work towards building a more financially secure and resilient society for all.

Lack of Financial Literacy

Lack of financial literacy is a significant problem many men face, often leading to poor financial decision-making, debt accumulation, and financial insecurity. Additionally, individuals may fall victim to financial scams or predatory lending practices because they lack knowledge about financial products and services. Furthermore, the lack of financial literacy can perpetuate cycles of poverty and inequality. Individuals from disadvantaged backgrounds may have limited access to financial education and resources, exacerbating their economic struggles. Without the necessary knowledge and skills to build wealth and achieve financial security, individuals may remain trapped in poverty, unable to break free from the cycle of financial hardship.

Financial literacy refers to understanding basic financial concepts, such as budgeting, saving, investing, and managing debt. With adequate financial literacy skills, men may be able to navigate the complexities of personal finance and make informed financial decisions. Gaining the skills to create and stick to a budget allows you to prioritize expenses, make informed decisions, save for the future, and avoid unnecessary debt and financial hardship. Understanding basic investment principles, such as risk and return, diversification, and compounding interest, gives you opportunities to grow wealth and achieve long-term financial goals.

Are you finding it difficult to achieve the financial dreams you're looking for?

Addressing this issue requires a concerted effort to improve financial education and literacy among individuals of all ages and backgrounds. By equipping men with the knowledge and skills needed to make informed financial decisions, we can empower them to achieve financial security, build wealth, and create a more financially resilient society for all.

Debt and Financial Stress

Debt and financial stress are significant problems that many men grapple with, often leading to stress, anxiety, strain on relationships, and an overall diminished quality of life. According to a financial survey on Forbes, 77% of Americans are dealing with debt.[43] Many accumulate debt through credit cards, student loans, mortgages, and medical bills. Loss of income or other unforeseen life events can cause us to get behind on our monthly payments, leading to late fees and higher interest rates. This results in a cycle of debt that can feel overwhelming and insurmountable.

Debt can have far-reaching consequences beyond just financial strain. Financial disagreements lead to arguments, resentment, and relationship breakdowns. According to the same Forbes survey, 54% of respondents said they often feel stressed because of their debt and that this financial stress led to:

- disagreements in relationships (59%)
- loss of trust from loved ones (55%)
- sleep difficulties (48%)
- increased anxiety (40%)
- a diminished social life (38%)
- depression (34%)

How is debt affecting you?

Debt can hinder individuals' ability to achieve their long-term financial goals and aspirations. It can limit opportunities for saving, investing, and building wealth, as individuals must allocate a significant portion of their income toward debt repayment. This can delay major life milestones, such as buying a home, starting a family, or saving for retirement, further exacerbating financial stress and insecurity. Debt and financial stress are pervasive problems that affect many men.

---

[43] Horton, Cassidy. "The Silent Strain: How Debt Takes a Toll on Mental Health." Edited by Michael Benninger. Forbes, October 2, 2023. https://www.forbes.com/advisor/banking/american-debt-and-the-mental-health-epidemic/.

When debt gets out of hand it puts an increased reliance on social welfare programs and support services to assist those facing financial hardship.

Addressing these issues requires a multifaceted approach, including improving financial literacy, promoting responsible borrowing and lending practices, and providing support and resources to those facing hardships. By empowering individuals to manage their finances effectively and make informed financial decisions, we can work towards reducing debt and economic stress and creating a more financially resilient society for all.

Unfulfilling Career Choices
Unfulfilling career choices represent a significant problem many men encounter, impacting their overall satisfaction, well-being, and sense of purpose. This issue arises when individuals find themselves in jobs or career paths that don't align with their interests, values, and aspirations, leaving them feeling unfulfilled, stagnant, and dissatisfied.

Many men may find themselves stuck in jobs with low wages, lack of opportunities for advancement, and poor management. Often, there is a disconnect between an individual's skills and passions and the demands of their jobs. As a result, they may feel uninspired, unmotivated, and disconnected from their work, leading to frustration and disillusionment. Feeling unfulfilled in your career can also have detrimental effects on mental health and overall well-being. In fact, research shows that stress and dissatisfaction at work can lead to burnout, anxiety, and depression.[44]

Unfulfilling career choices can hinder individuals' personal and professional growth, limiting their potential for advancement

---

[44] Nadinloyi, Karim Babayi, Hasan Sadeghi, and Nader Hajloo. "Relationship between Job Satisfaction and Employees Mental Health." *Procedia - Social and Behavioral Sciences* 84 (July 2013): 293–97. https://doi.org/10.1016/j.sbspro.2013.06.554.

and success. When individuals are not engaged or motivated in their work, they may become complacent and stagnant, failing to develop new skills, pursue growth opportunities, or take on new challenges. This can result in missed opportunities for career advancement, increased job insecurity, and a lack of fulfillment in both personal and professional life.

These unfulfilling career choices can impact relationships and social connections. Individuals may feel disconnected from their social networks due to their lack of enthusiasm or engagement in their work. Moreover, dissatisfaction with one's career can spill over into other areas of life, leading to damaged relationships and adverse family outcomes.

If there were no barriers, what would you choose to do for a career and why?

Planning for the Future

Many men face the significant problem of being unable to plan for the future, which often leads to uncertainty, financial insecurity, and missed opportunities. This issue arises when individuals fail to set goals, establish priorities, and take proactive steps to prepare for upcoming challenges and opportunities. Without a roadmap for success, individuals may miss out on opportunities for advancement, skill development, and career progression. The inability to plan for the future can harm financial security and stability, leaving you vulnerable to unexpected expenses and other setbacks.

Addressing this issue requires a proactive approach to goal setting, financial planning, and personal development. However, with specific goals or objectives to work towards, you can make meaningful progress in your personal or professional life. With a strategic financial plan, you can save for emergencies, invest for retirement, or plan for significant life milestones such as buying a home or starting a family. By encouraging individuals to clarify their goals, establish priorities, and take proactive steps to prepare for the future, we can work towards creating a society where everyone has the opportunity to achieve their full potential and thrive.

The Bible and Money

Before delving into solutions for debt management and increasing income, examining the Bible's profound insights regarding money is essential. One of the most commonly quoted verses on this subject is 1 Timothy 6:10, which cautions: "For the love of money is the root of all evil: which while some coveted after, they have erred from the faith, and pierced themselves through with many sorrows."

Individuals frequently misinterpret Bible verses, distorting their true meanings and causing confusion among believers and non-believers alike. Take, for instance, the familiar phrase, "money is the root of all evil," from the book of Timothy. The actual quote is, "The LOVE of money is A root of all sorts of evil." Money itself isn't inherently evil; the unhealthy obsession with wealth is the real problem.

We must guard against becoming excessively fixated on wealth, ensuring that our love for God supersedes any attachment to material possessions. Hebrews 13:5 advises that we should strive to liberate ourselves from materialism's grip and find contentment in what we already possess, trusting that God will never forsake us. Cultivating inner contentment is crucial for navigating this godly path, allowing those who seek the Lord to find satisfaction in every circumstance while avoiding envy and greed.

How are you glorifying the Kingdom with the money you make?

Let's face it: money frequently brings stress into our lives, especially concerning providing for our families and managing our finances. It's imperative to prioritize seeking the Kingdom of God and living righteously, trusting that God will help us meet our needs. God created a world filled with abundant resources, and he wants us to enjoy all he has given us.

Importantly, the accumulation and utilization of money provide an opportunity to tithe and give back, as commanded in Scripture in Malachi 3:10: "Bring ye all the tithes into the storehouse, that there may be meat in mine house, and prove me now herewith, saith the LORD of hosts, if I will not open you the windows of heaven, and pour you out a blessing, that there shall not be room enough to receive it."

Proverbs 11:25 instructs us that "a generous person will prosper" and "whoever refreshes others will be refreshed." This fundamental principle underscores the wisdom of adhering to God's guidelines for managing our finances. Following a Biblical worldview of our finances and money will allow us a world of riches far beyond the accumulation of money.

Financial Education

Financial education can help to address the pervasive problem of economic instability and financial illiteracy among men. It encompasses the knowledge, skills, and resources necessary to make informed financial decisions, manage money effectively, and achieve financial well-being. By providing access to financial education, we can empower men to take control of their finances, build wealth, and secure their future.

One of the primary benefits of financial education is its ability to equip individuals with the knowledge and skills needed to navigate the complexities of personal finance. Through financial education programs, individuals can learn about fundamental concepts such as:

- budgeting
- saving
- investing
- and managing debt

Are you currently setting financial goals for your family?

Financial education is crucial in promoting responsible financial behavior and reducing the risk of financial pitfalls such as overspending, impulse buying, and debt accumulation. Financial education empowers you to make better choices by developing essential critical thinking skills to assess various financial options' costs, benefits, and risks. When you can make informed financial decisions, you can minimize potential risks and build financial security.

Also, financial education promotes financial independence and self-reliance by teaching individuals how to take control of their finances and plan for their future. By learning how to set financial goals, develop a savings plan, and create a personalized financial roadmap, individuals can take proactive steps to achieve their financial objectives and build a secure financial future for themselves and their families.

Through increased financial literacy and knowledge, individuals can build a secure financial future for themselves and their families, contributing to overall economic stability and prosperity.

Budgeting and Saving Strategies

Budgeting and saving strategies offer practical solutions to the challenges of financial instability and uncertainty, providing individuals with the tools and techniques needed to manage their money effectively, achieve their financial goals, and build wealth over time. These strategies involve creating a plan for how money will be allocated and saved, allowing individuals to prioritize expenses, reduce unnecessary spending, and increase savings for future needs and goals.

One of the primary benefits of budgeting and saving strategies is their ability to provide individuals with a clear roadmap for managing their finances. By creating a budget, individuals can track their income and expenses, identify areas where they may be overspending, and adjust their spending to meet their financial goals and priorities. This can help individuals gain control over their finances, reduce financial stress, and make informed decisions about allocating resources.

1. Create a long-term strategy.
2. Set spending limits and avoid impulse buys.
3. Save a portion of your monthly pay to build a financial cushion to protect against unexpected expenses and emergencies.

You should also consider budgeting and saving strategies that help you achieve short-term and long-term financial goals, such as buying a home, starting a business, or saving for retirement. By setting specific savings goals and regularly contributing to a savings account or investment portfolio, individuals can progress steadily toward their objectives and build a secure financial future for themselves and their families.

Budgeting and saving strategies promote financial discipline and self-control by encouraging individuals to prioritize spending and resist impulse purchases. By distinguishing between needs and wants and making conscious choices about allocating resources, you can develop healthy financial habits and avoid unnecessary spending that derails financial plans.

The strategies you develop can have a positive ripple effect that extends beyond the individual level to impact families, communities, and society as a whole. Families may experience increased financial stability and well-being as a result of improved budgeting and saving habits, leading to reduced financial stress and tension in the household.

Budgeting and saving strategies offer practical solutions to the challenges of financial instability and uncertainty, empowering men to take control of their finances, achieve their financial goals, and build wealth over time. By implementing these strategies, men can gain control over their finances, reduce financial stress, and build a secure financial future for themselves and their families, contributing to overall economic stability and prosperity.

Debt Management

Debt management is a crucial solution for men facing the challenges of financial instability and debt accumulation, offering practical strategies to regain control over their finances, reduce debt burden, and achieve long-term financial stability. Debt management involves implementing strategies to effectively manage and pay off existing debt while preventing the accumulation of new debt, allowing individuals to regain financial independence and peace of mind.

One of the primary benefits of debt management is its ability to provide individuals with a structured plan for paying off debt and becoming debt-free. By assessing their current financial situation, including total debt balances, interest rates, and monthly payments, individuals can develop a personalized debt repayment plan tailored to their unique circumstances. This plan may involve prioritizing high-interest debts, such as credit card balances, and making extra payments to pay down debt more quickly.

Plus, reducing debt can help individuals negotiate with creditors to lower interest rates, reduce monthly payments, or establish more manageable repayment terms. By communicating openly and honestly with creditors about their financial difficulties, individuals may be able to secure concessions that make debt repayment more affordable and sustainable over time. This can help alleviate financial stress and prevent the escalation of debt problems in the future.

Managing debt fosters financial responsibility and account-ability, urging individuals to take proactive measures to break free from the cycle of debt accumulation.

Debt management strategies:

- Commit to living within your means.
- Avoid unnecessary spending and impulse buys
- Put aside a little each month towards debt repayment.

Debt strategies can help individuals develop healthy financial habits and behaviors that promote long-term financial well-being. By learning how to budget effectively, prioritize spending, and save for emergencies, individuals can build a strong financial foundation that protects against future financial setbacks and reduces the risk of falling back into debt.

Is your current career purpose filled?

Pursuing Purpose-filled Careers

One of the primary benefits of pursuing fulfilling careers is its ability to enhance overall job satisfaction and well-being. When individuals engage in work that they find meaningful and reward-ing, they are more likely to experience a sense of fulfillment, purpose, and satisfaction in their daily lives. This can lead to increased motivation, enthusiasm, and productivity in the work-place, ultimately resulting in higher levels of job satisfaction and overall well-being.

A fulfilling career allows individuals to leverage their unique talents, skills, and passions to make a positive impact in their chosen field or industry. By aligning their career goals with their personal values and interests, individuals can find opportunities to contribute meaningfully to their work and society, leading to a sense of pride, accomplishment, and fulfillment in their professional lives.

Finding your calling and having a fulfilling career is a crucial solution for men seeking to overcome the challenges of dissatisfaction and stagnation in the workplace, offering opportunities for personal growth, professional development, and overall well-being. By actively seeking out career paths and opportunities that align with their interests, values, and aspirations, individuals can find purpose, satisfaction, and fulfillment in their work. Improvements at work ultimately lead to greater happiness, success, and well-being in all aspects of their lives.

Long-Term Financial Planning

Long-term financial planning is vital for men aiming to secure their financial future, build wealth, and achieve their life goals. This approach involves creating a strategic financial roadmap that outlines specific objectives, identifies potential challenges, and establishes actionable steps to achieve desired outcomes over an extended period.

One significant benefit of long-term financial planning is its ability to provide individuals with a clear vision and direction for their financial journey. By setting long-term goals, such as retirement savings, homeownership, or funding education, individuals can establish a framework for making informed financial decisions and prioritizing their resources accordingly.

Do you currently have long-term financial planning goals?

Creating long-term financial planning enables individuals to anticipate and mitigate potential risks and challenges that may arise over time. By conducting a thorough assessment of their financial situation and identifying potential obstacles, such as market volatility, inflation, or unexpected expenses, individuals can develop strategies to protect their assets and safeguard their financial well-being.

Financial planning promotes disciplined saving and investing habits that can lead to the accumulation of wealth over time. By consistently setting aside funds for savings and investment purposes, individuals can take advantage of compounding returns and grow their assets exponentially, allowing them to achieve their long-term financial goals more efficiently.

Additionally, long-term financial planning provides individuals with peace of mind and financial security, knowing they have a plan to achieve their goals and weather any financial storms that may arise. By taking proactive steps to prepare for the future, individuals can reduce uncertainty and anxiety about their financial well-being, allowing them to focus on other aspects of their lives with confidence and peace of mind.

Finally, long-term financial planning is crucial for men seeking to secure their financial future, build wealth, and achieve their life goals. By creating a strategic financial roadmap and taking proactive steps to prepare for the future, individuals can increase their financial security, reduce uncertainty, and achieve greater peace of mind and well-being in all aspects of their lives.

Getting Your Finances Right
To achieve financial stability and promote mental well-being, it's essential to take actionable steps toward managing finances effectively. This involves creating a budget to track income and expenses, prioritizing saving for emergencies and long-term goals, and managing debt responsibly. By establishing financial goals and developing a plan to achieve them, individuals can

reduce financial stress and increase feelings of security and control over their finances.

Seeking out financial education and resources can provide valuable insights and strategies for improving financial literacy and decision-making. Learning how to budget effectively, invest wisely, and plan for the future can empower individuals to make informed financial choices and achieve greater financial stability over time.

It's important to prioritize self-care and seek support when needed to manage stress and promote mental well-being. Practicing mindfulness, engaging in regular physical activity, and maintaining a healthy work-life balance can all contribute to overall wellness and resilience in the face of financial challenges.

By recognizing the relationship between financial stability and mental well-being and taking proactive steps to address financial challenges, men can achieve greater overall happiness and fulfillment in their lives. By prioritizing financial education, responsible money management, and self-care, men can build a solid foundation for a brighter and more secure future.

Scan the code above with your smartphone
to view my chapter wrap-up video.

Go to this link to access the Chapter Worksheets:
https://truemanlifecoaching.com/TrueManTrueWaysWorksheets

Rest Stop

Journal and reflect on your thoughts concerning financial empowerment. Think about what it will take to achieve financial success and move you toward becoming the True Man you want to be.

_____

_____

_____

_____

_____

_____

_____

_____

_____

_____

_____

_____

_____

_____

_____

_____

_____

_____

_____

MIKE VAN PELT

Chapter Twelve

Gear Up for Greatness: Leadership and Responsibility

True Man Tip

A leader is someone who has a unique vision of the future. They are able to perceive beyond the ordinary because they have a heightened awareness, foresight, and a proactive approach to responsibilities.

I enjoy Indy car racing and open-wheel racing as you learned earlier. There is a lot of activity when a driver is in the cockpit leading his or her team. The average Indianapolis 500-mile race takes about 3 hours, and how the driver cares for the car is critically important.

One aspect that a driver must perform in the car is shifting gears. Shifting gears affects the car in several ways. It alters the power delivery, allowing the driver to harness the engine's torque across different speed ranges. Shifting gears also influence the car's acceleration and top speed capabilities, enabling it to reach optimal velocity on straightaways and navigate corners more effectively. In addition, shifting impacts the car's balance and stability, affecting traction and handling through turns and under braking.

I love Indy racing, and I believe it can teach us a lot about leadership. A skilled driver uses their hard-won skills and foresight to guide the car across the finish line. They intuitively know which gears to shift and when. Once they master their vehicle and the track, you know your driver is ready to win big in the Indy 500.

Do you have a winning formula for life?

If you observe the leaders around you, you can discover the subtle differences that separate a good leader from a great one. While leadership is often associated with roles like CEO, head coach, or national leader, it transcends mere positions; it's fundamentally a skill. Leadership is about positively influencing others, whether guiding your children, supporting your spouse, or nurturing your family, just as much as leading others or organizations personally or professionally.

In the journey toward personal and professional excellence, you must master the twin pillars of leadership and responsibility. This is the key to unlocking the doors to unprecedented success and fulfillment. Brace yourself, for the leadership transformation begins now.

Addressing the Leadership Problem

Imagine a world where leaders are scarce. What does it look like? It's a world where responsibilities are shunned, decisions linger in uncertainty, motivation is a distant dream, and challenges paralyze progress. (No, this is not our present world, but it feels like it.)

The problems are real, and they hinder the very essence of personal growth and accomplishment. In today's rapidly evolving landscape, the call for leadership and responsibility amongst men, both personally and professionally, has never been more critical. Now, more than ever, men are called upon to rise to the occasion by taking charge of their lives and learning to lead with integrity and purpose.

At its core, leadership begins with oneself. It requires a deep understanding of one's strengths, weaknesses, values, and beliefs. It demands self-awareness and self-discipline. As men, we must first lead ourselves before we can lead others. This means taking ownership of our actions, holding ourselves accountable for our decisions, and continuously striving for self-improvement. It's about setting high standards and living up to them daily, even when faced with adversity or temptation.

Leadership extends beyond individual growth; it encompasses our interactions with others and the impact we have on our communities and organizations. In our professional lives, this means stepping up to the plate, taking on challenges, and inspiring those around us to achieve greatness. It means fostering a culture of collaboration, respect, and innovation, where every team member feels valued and empowered to contribute their best work. Authentic leadership isn't about exerting power or authority; it's about serving others, lifting them up, and helping them reach their full potential.

Are you lifting others up to reach their full potential?

With great leadership comes great responsibility. As men, we must recognize the weight of our decisions and the ripple effect they can have on those around us. This means considering the long-term implications of our behavior. It means being a role model for integrity, honesty, and accountability in our personal and professional lives. It's up to us to ensure that our actions positively influence those around us.

Yet, despite the importance of leadership and responsibility, many men still need help to fully embrace these principles. Perhaps they don't know that leadership is a skill and a mindset that can be developed and honed over time. How?

- Learn how to step outside of your comfort zone

- Seek out a quality mentor
- Invest in your personal development

The need for leadership and responsibility amongst men has never been greater. In a world filled with uncertainty and challenges, it's up to us to rise to the occasion, to lead with integrity and purpose, and to inspire those around us to do the same. By cultivating self-awareness, embracing accountability, and serving others with humility and compassion, we can become the leaders our families, communities, and workplaces desperately need. The time for action is now; let us seize the opportunity to make a difference and leave a legacy worth remembering.

Unlocking Leadership Potential

At the heart of our pursuit lies the primary obstacle – the scarcity of leadership skills. Genuine leadership isn't just a title; it's a skill set that demands cultivation and refinement. Let's dive deep into the intricacies of leadership development, dissecting the characteristics that set exceptional leaders apart.

Leadership isn't about barking orders; it's about igniting inspiration and guiding individuals toward a common goal. Effective leaders possess an intimate understanding of their team or family members, acknowledging their strengths and weaknesses. Through empathetic leadership, they foster trust, cultivating an environment where collaboration flourishes.

Are you including others, or are you a lone ranger?

A leader is a perpetual student. This segment of our road trip equips you with the tools to sharpen your communication prowess, a cornerstone of effective leadership. Learn to express your thoughts clearly, engage in active listening, and adapt your communication style to resonate with diverse audiences.

The journey doesn't halt there. Authentic leadership transcends self-interest; it's about serving others. Uncover the essence of servant leadership, where the focus shifts from personal gain to the collective welfare and advancement of the team. Unveil the potency of leading by example, for actions speak volumes in the realm of leadership.

As we navigate the nuances of leadership development, remember that these skills aren't confined to the boardroom. They intertwine with your personal life, enriching your relationships and catalyzing positive change within your community.

Leadership isn't a static endpoint; it's an ongoing odyssey of growth, education, and service. Prepare yourself as we peel back the layers of leadership development, empowering you to lead with authenticity and influence.

Leadership Development: Unlocking Your Potential

Embarking on the journey of leadership development is like discovering a treasure trove within yourself. It's a process that requires introspection, self-awareness, and a commitment to growth. To unlock your potential as a leader, you must first understand your own strengths and weaknesses.

This self-awareness lays the foundation for effective leadership, allowing you to leverage your strengths while proactively addressing areas for improvement. Effective leadership isn't about exerting authority or dictating orders; it's about inspiring others to action, guiding them toward a shared vision, and fostering a collaborative environment where everyone can thrive. It requires empathy, understanding, and the ability to connect with people on a deeper level.

Central to effective leadership is the mastery of communication. Clear, concise communication is essential for conveying ideas, building trust, and aligning team members toward common goals. As a leader, you must hone your communication skills by learning to articulate your thoughts effectively, actively listening to others, and adapting your message to resonate with diverse audiences. Effective communication fosters transparency, encourages collaboration, and strengthens relationships within the team.

Are you clear in your communication?

A true leader is constantly seeking out new knowledge, perspectives, and experiences to broaden their understanding and refine their skills. Whether through formal education, mentorship, or hands-on experience, the journey of leadership development is one of constant evolution and refinement.

Effective leadership is about serving others and fostering a culture of empowerment and growth within the team. This requires humility, empathy, and a willingness to put the needs of others before your own. By leading with integrity, authenticity, and a genuine concern for the well-being of your family or team members at work, you can inspire loyalty, trust, and commitment.

Leadership development is a transformative journey that involves unlocking your potential, mastering the art of communication, and cultivating a mindset of continuous learning and growth. It's about understanding yourself, inspiring others, and creating an environment where everyone can thrive. By embracing the principles of effective leadership and committing to your own personal and professional development, you can unlock your true potential as a leader and make a lasting impact on those around you.

Why Does Leadership Development Matter?

Leadership development matters because it's the pathway to unlocking one's full potential and making a meaningful impact in both personal and professional areas of life. It's a recognition that leadership is not an innate trait reserved for a select few, but rather a skill set that can be honed and cultivated over time. By investing in leadership development, individuals equip themselves with the tools necessary to navigate the complexities of the modern world, inspire others, and drive positive change.

Understanding one's leadership style is central to effective leadership development. Whether one leans towards being a visionary, a democratic leader, or a servant leader, recognizing and embracing one's unique approach is essential. Great leaders aren't carbon copies of each other; they're authentic individuals who understand their strengths and weaknesses and are able to lead with authenticity and integrity. By knowing one's leadership style, individuals can lead with confidence, making decisions that align with their values and resonate with those they lead.

How are you developing your leadership skills?

Leadership development empowers individuals to navigate challenges and uncertainty with resilience and grace. In today's rapidly changing world, leaders must be adaptable, innovative, and confident in navigating complex situations. If you can master these qualities, you'll be better equipped to tackle challenges head-on, turn setbacks into opportunities, and lead your family or work teams to success.

Key leadership qualities:[45]

1. Authenticity
2. Problem-solving
3. Decision-making
4. Adaptability

---

[45] Some of these qualities were taken from this article: Knight, Rebecca. "8 Essential Qualities of Successful Leaders." *Harvard Business Review*. Harvard Business Review, December 13, 2023. https://hbr.org/2023/12/8-essential-qualities-of-successful-leaders.

5. Communication: Being Clear and Concise
6. Practicing Empathy
7. Emotional intelligence
8. Resilience

In addition, focus on the following two qualities:

1. Practice empathy. When you practice empathy, you're putting yourself in the other person's shoes to understand their perspective. Acknowledge their feelings and respond with empathy, such as saying, "I can see why you feel that way." Empathy strengthens connections and helps resolve conflicts more effectively.
2. Be clear and concise in your communication. Communicate your thoughts clearly and avoid overcomplicating your message. Stick to the point and be specific about your needs or expectations. Clear and concise communication reduces confusion and ensures that your message is understood.

Effectively building these communication skills will help you develop deeper and more meaningful relationships with the people in your life. It will also cause a ripple effect of growth for those you lead. Being heard and valued will inspire others to pass it onto the people they lead.

Finally, leadership development empowers individuals to lead authentically, navigate challenges confidently, and inspire others to achieve greatness. It can also contribute to the growth and success of your teams, organizations, and communities. In a world where we need effective leadership more than ever, leadership development is not just important — it's essential.

How Can Leadership Development Help You

Leadership development skills are invaluable assets that extend their benefits beyond the confines of the workplace, permeating into the fabric of our personal lives. Effective leadership isn't a rigid mold but a dynamic set of strategies and techniques tailored to fit different contexts and demands. By mastering the intricacies of leadership, individuals guide others toward success and cultivate an environment where innovation and success flourish.

Effective leadership is the cornerstone of a thriving workplace and family culture. Picture an environment where everyone feels empowered to contribute their best ideas. This is the result of effective leadership in action. When leaders understand their own strengths and weaknesses, as well as those of their team members, they can harness this knowledge to create an atmosphere of trust, respect, and inclusivity. In such an environment, employees and families are more engaged, motivated, and committed to achieving shared goals, which increases productivity and organizational success.

The impact of effective leadership extends beyond the workplace and into our personal relationships. The same principles that drive successful leadership — empathy, communication, and adaptability — are equally essential in fostering strong and meaningful connections with family, friends, and loved ones.

By leading with empathy and understanding, individuals can navigate conflicts, communicate effectively, and cultivate a supportive and nurturing environment at home. Whether it's resolving conflicts with a partner, communicating effectively with children, or collaborating with extended family members, practical leadership skills are invaluable tools that enhance the quality of our personal relationships.

Embracing responsibility is a natural extension of effective leadership. Leaders understand the importance of accountability and take ownership of their actions, decisions, and impact on others. It's about taking proactive steps to address challenges, overcome obstacles, and drive positive change within oneself and the broader community.

How do you embrace responsibility?

As we go deeper into the exploration of leadership develop-ment, let us remember its transformative power and ability to enrich every aspect of our lives. So, let us embrace the journey of growth, empowerment, and responsibility, knowing that the skills we cultivate will benefit us and those around us, both professionally and personally.

Embracing Responsibility: The Catalyst for Personal Growth

Embracing responsibility means recognizing that our every action has consequences. It's about understanding the impact of our choices on ourselves and those around us. Embracing responsibility means taking ownership of our actions, mistakes, and successes.

When something goes wrong, do you take responsibility or run from it?

In your personal growth, remember that we are the architects of our own lives with the help of God. We have the power to shape our destinies through the choices we make and the actions we take. When we become active participants in our own evolution, we can become the best versions of ourselves.

Embracing responsibility in our personal lives means honoring our commitments to ourselves and to others. It's about showing up, putting in the effort, and following through on our promises, even when it's not convenient or easy. Whether it's sticking to a fitness routine, pursuing a passion project, or nurturing our relationships, responsibility grounds us in integrity and self-discipline, laying the foundation for success and fulfillment.

We must acknowledge the impact of our choices on ourselves and those around us. It's about recognizing that we have agency in shaping our own destinies and that our actions have consequences. Whether it's taking ownership of our health and well-being, nurturing our relationships, or pursuing our passions, accepting responsibility gives us accountability and self-awareness. It enables us to make intentional choices that align with our values and aspirations, leading to a more fulfilling and purpose-driven life.

Responsibility in the Professional Realm

In our professional lives, we must take ownership of our roles by striving for excellence in everything we do. The best leaders lead by example, demonstrating integrity, accountability, and a commitment to the collective success of their teams. They understand that their actions set the tone for the entire organization and that true leadership requires humility, empathy, and a willingness to listen and learn.

As in our personal lives, we must recognize the impact of our decisions on the broader community. It's about considering not just the bottom line but also the ethical implications of our actions and the welfare of everyone involved. Responsible leaders prioritize sustainability, diversity, and social responsibility.

How do you practice empathy in your life?

Great leaders understand that success is not just about profits and growth but also about making a positive impact on the world around us. They inspire trust and confidence in our colleagues, clients, and stakeholders, fostering a culture of integrity and accountability within our organizations.

In essence, embracing responsibility in our personal and professional lives is essential for achieving growth, success, and fulfillment. It empowers us to take control of our destinies, learn from our experiences, and positively impact the world around us.

An Everyday Example of Leadership Excellence

Peter is a manager at a marketing company who oversees a team. He is known for demonstrating integrity, accountability, and a deep commitment to his team's success. Peter knows his department is affected by his leadership, and that means his behavior must be consistent with the principles he holds dear.

One day, Peter's group is focusing on a significant campaign for a high-profile customer. The project has a short timeline and significant risks. As the project develops, Peter discovers that Amy, one of the team members, made a mistake in the data analysis that might have disastrous effects on the campaign. Rather than criticizing or accusing her, Peter handles the matter with humility and kindness.

As the team's leader, Peter calls a meeting and candidly addresses the mistake, taking ownership of the situation. Peter emphasizes that errors are inevitable and that what counts is how they resolve them as a team. Amy is reassured by him that the error is a chance for improvement rather than a reflection of her shortcomings. By handling the situation quietly and constructively Peter sets a good example for his colleagues and fosters a safe workplace where they feel supported rather than blamed.

To ensure the campaign stays on track, Peter rolls up his sleeves and works alongside the team to correct the error. He encourages teamwork by listening to everyone's opinions and valuing their contributions. The team has more faith in Peter's leadership because of his readiness to grow and change as a result of the circumstances. They are aware that he cares about how they work as a team to accomplish their goals as well as the final product.

Lead Like a True Man

There are numerous leadership accounts in the Bible, but when you write a book about becoming a True Man, there is only one person to look at as the ultimate role model: Jesus Christ. If you're a Christian, then it's obvious that Jesus is the ultimate leader. He leads heaven and earth, plain and simple.

Jesus interacted with people in a transformative manner, serving them in a way that profoundly impacted their lives. His dedication to freeing people exemplified His role as a servant leader.

Following Jesus' teachings and cultivating a personal relationship with Him transforms individuals into better versions of themselves than they could achieve independently. Jesus emphasized that this is the essence of servant leadership — the only model He advocated.

What did Jesus teach us about leadership and accountability?

Jesus set a standard that transcends time and culture. Through his actions and words, Jesus exemplified three key traits of servant leadership:

1. Humility
2. Selflessness
3. A commitment to serving others

Jesus demonstrated humility in its purest form. Despite being the Son of God, he willingly took on the role of a servant by washing his disciples' feet — a profound act of humility and service. His willingness to perform the most menial tasks without seeking recognition or status exemplifies true humility. In a world often obsessed with power and prestige, Jesus' humility is a powerful reminder that true leadership begins with a humble heart.

Jesus prioritized the needs of others above his own. He consistently placed the well-being of others ahead of his comfort or convenience, demonstrating selflessness in action. Whether he was healing the sick, feeding the hungry, or comforting the broken-hearted, Jesus' selfless acts of service reflected his deep compassion and concern for humanity. His example challenges us to consider the needs of others and to sacrifice our selfish desires in order to serve them with love and compassion.

Jesus exhibited empathy and compassion towards all people. He saw the struggles of those around him, and responded with compassion and kindness. Jesus welcomed the marginalized, the outcasts, and the sinners, showing them love and acceptance. His empathy towards others demonstrated the transformative power of compassion. In a world marked by division and indifference, Jesus' example of empathy challenges leaders to cultivate compassion and understanding towards all people, regardless of their background or circumstances.

Jesus fostered a culture of empowerment and growth among his followers. He invested in the development of his disciples, equipping them with the knowledge, skills, and confidence they needed to fulfill their potential. Jesus entrusted his disciples with responsibilities, empowered them to make decisions, and encouraged them to step out in faith. His commitment to empowering others underscores the essence of servant leadership, which is centered on lifting others up and helping them succeed.

Lastly, Jesus led by example, modeling the servant leadership principles he taught. He lived out his values with integrity and consistency, earning the trust and respect of those around him. Jesus' life was a testament to the power of servant leadership in action, inspiring countless individuals to follow in his footsteps. His unwavering commitment to serving others, coupled with his humility, selflessness, empathy, and empowerment, solidify his legacy as the ultimate example of great leadership.

Jesus' life and teachings provide a roadmap for servant leadership. His humility, selflessness, empathy, empowerment, and exemplary leadership serve as a model for leaders in every sphere of life. By emulating the servant leadership traits exhibited by Jesus, leaders can cultivate healthier organizations, build stronger communities, and make a positive impact on the world. As the greatest leadership example ever, Jesus continues to inspire and challenge leaders to lead with humility, compassion, and a servant's heart.

If you want to become the best leader in life, there is only one way to do it, and Jesus provides it when He says, "Follow Me."

Become More Christ-Like

Jesus provides us with a roadmap on how to become more like him. We can learn a lot from His leadership. First, ask God for help. Jesus said, "Ask me anything in my name, and I'll do it" (John 14:14). So, pray for it, and God's got your back.

Second, study Jesus. The Gospels clearly lay out Christ's life, and the New Testament adds more teachings from His disciples. Even the Old Testament provides much information regarding the prophecies related to Jesus Christ. Dive into the Bible, and you'll see how to live a servant leadership life.

Third, put His teachings into action. James said, "Don't just listen to the word; do what it says" (James 1:22). Treat others right, especially the downtrodden. Christ's big on love, so show it.

Fourth, find some role models. Paul said, "Follow my lead, as I follow the example of Christ" (1 Corinthians 11:1). Hang around folks who walk the talk.

Fifth, lean on your Christian community. Hebrews says, "Encourage each other to love and do good" (Hebrews 10:24-25). When you lift each other up, you all get stronger.

And there's more wisdom in the Bible. James says, "Get close to God, and He'll get close to you" (James 4:8). Plus, sharing in Christ's suffering makes you more like Him (Philippians 3:10-11).

The bottom line is, if you want to become a True Man, you should aim to be more like Christ. Follow these steps, and you'll get there and make a real difference in the world.

Scan the code above with your smartphone
to view my chapter wrap-up video.

Go to this link to access the Chapter Worksheets:
https://truemanlifecoaching.com/TrueManTrueWaysWorksheets

Rest Stop

Journal and reflect on your thoughts concerning leadership and responsibility and how it can move you toward becoming the True Man you want to be.

_____

_____

_____

_____

_____

_____

_____

_____

_____

_____

_____

_____

_____

_____

_____

_____

_____

_____

_____

_____

Chapter Thirteen

Destination Legacy and Impact

True Man Tip

*What truly defines our legacy isn't merely the
duration of our life, but rather the extent of
our influence and the lasting impact we leave behind.*

Several years ago, I attended a training program where we were tasked with writing our own eulogies. This eulogy prompt encouraged us to ponder our desired legacy, aiming to guide us to live with greater focus and purpose. It was emotionally challenging to write. Writing about my life in this way was cathartic because it unveiled a path toward genuine freedom I hadn't previously recognized. But I was also terrified by the work needed to build a lasting legacy. This is a place where many men find themselves.

How would you like your eulogy to read?

How do you wish to be remembered? What impact do you aspire to leave on others' lives and careers? This chapter gives you the tools and techniques to help you define your legacy and clarify your values and aspirations.

When you think about securing a legacy for your family, you might picture the tangible: wealth, investments, or property — all those things measured in digits and square footage. Yet, in the grand scheme, they're just that: things. While they may provide a safety net for those we leave behind, they lack the depth of what defines a legacy. I believe it's about imparting values, wisdom, and a way of life transcending the physical realm. It's the intangible imprint we leave on the hearts and minds of our loved ones — the lessons learned, the stories shared, the principles lived by.

So, as we ponder our legacies, let's not merely focus on family heirlooms but also on the richness of character and the depth of relationships we cultivate. For, in the end, it's only these intangible treasures that endure beyond the passing of time. As we delve into determining our personal legacies, let us look again to Jesus as our role model.

Jesus and His Legacy

Jesus Christ stands as one of history's most influential figures, leaving an indelible mark on humanity that transcends religious boundaries. At the core of his teachings lies a message of love, forgiveness, and compassion — which has resonated throughout the ages, shaping individual lives and societal values.

The fundamental principle of valuing every human life, irrespective of background, underscores the universality of Jesus's teachings and serves as a timeless guide for humanity. The profound impact of Jesus's message is evident in its transformative power, inspiring believers to emulate his example of selflessness and compassion.

How can you be more like Jesus?

Jesus's ethical teachings, encapsulated in the Golden Rule — "Do unto others as you would have them do unto you" — have profoundly shaped moral philosophy and ethical thought. This principle, rooted in compassion and empathy, serves as a guiding light for individuals and societies alike, prompting the pursuit of justice, equality, and human dignity.

Living Christ-like is not merely an act of religious devotion but a pathway to building a meaningful legacy. By embodying the principles of love, forgiveness, and compassion espoused by Jesus, individuals can leave a lasting impact on the world around them. Embracing the values of empathy, kindness, and social justice enables individuals to cultivate meaningful relationships, foster positive change, and leave behind a legacy of integrity and compassion. In essence, by following in the footsteps of Jesus, individuals can build a legacy that transcends their own lifetimes, shaping a brighter and more compassionate future for generations to come.

We can learn from Jesus that there is no shortcut to legacy. Jesus died on the cross to offer us complete salvation. Jesus instructed, demonstrated, and prepared His disciples to pass on and spread the good works of God, which continue to this day. Year after year, the Bible continues to be the number one book sold worldwide, and for good reason. The legacy of Jesus lives on, but the real question is, does He live on through you?

The Challenges of Creating a Long-Term Vision of the Future

Many of us find ourselves entangled in the web of day-to-day tasks, which leaves us little time to envision a long-term future. This lack of a forward-looking perspective can lead to a sense of drifting through life without a clear destination. It's not just about setting goals; it's about creating a vivid, compelling image of the legacy you want to leave behind.

The absence of a long-term vision can result in a reactive rather than a proactive approach to life. Do you react to challenges without considering how your actions contribute to a larger, more impactful narrative?

Imagine yourself cruising down a winding road, encountering twists and turns at every corner. Instead of using your GPS, you follow your impulses and see where the journey takes you.

But now, you're drifting aimlessly, left at the mercy of the road's unpredictability. This lack of direction can leave you feeling lost, unfulfilled, and unsure of the legacy you'll ultimately leave behind.

But it doesn't have to be this way. If you take the time to craft a profound and inspiring long-term vision, you can navigate life's challenges with purpose and determination. Whether you aspire to build a successful business, make a difference in your community, or leave a lasting impact on future generations, your vision will serve as the foundation upon which you build your legacy.

So, grab the steering wheel of life and prepare to chart a course toward your destiny. By crafting a compelling long-term vision, you'll transform from a passive bystander into the architect of your own future. With purpose as your compass, you'll navigate the seas of life with confidence, resilience, and an unwavering commitment to leaving behind a legacy that truly matters.

Solutions to Creating a Long-Term Vision

To create your long-term vision, you have to go deep. You must take the time to explore the values and principles that define who you are and the legacy you want to leave. Through practical exercises and thought-provoking questions, you'll gain clarity on your life's purpose and the impact you aim to have.

What plans are you creating for your life and legacy?

In your journal, write the following questions:

- What drives you?
- What brings you joy and fulfillment?
- What legacy do you wish to leave behind for future generations?

- What steps can you take today to move closer to your desired destination?
- How can you align your daily actions with your long-term vision?

But creating a long-term vision is not a one-time event; it's an ongoing process of refinement and adjustment. As you navigate through life's twists and turns, you may find that your priorities shift or your goals evolve. And that's okay. The key is to remain flexible and adaptable, to embrace change as an opportunity for growth and self-discovery.

Defining your personal legacy is a journey of self-discovery and empowerment. Through introspection, goal-setting, and a willingness to embrace change, you can create a legacy reflecting your true essence and the values you hold dear.

How to Define Personal Legacy

What do you want to be remembered for? What kind of mark do you want to leave on the world when you're gone? These are profound questions that many men struggle to answer. However, once you understand the true meaning of legacy, you can take the first steps toward fulfilling your true purpose. Your legacy transcends mere accomplishments; it's intricately woven with the fabric of your values, principles, and beliefs.

As we discussed in our chapter about vulnerability, many men are socialized to prioritize stoicism by suppressing their emotions. These ingrained expectations can create barriers to introspection and self-expression, making it challenging for men to openly explore their values, beliefs, and aspirations. Instead of embracing their authentic selves, men may feel compelled to conform to society's narrow definitions of success and masculinity.

Have you ever felt like this?
How did it affect you?

Life, in general, can also hinder men's ability to define their personal legacy. With endless distractions, obligations, and responsibilities vying for attention, carving out time for self-reflection and introspection can seem like a luxury reserved for the privileged few. In the hustle and bustle of daily life, the deeper questions of purpose can get pushed to the wayside, leaving men feeling disconnected from their true selves and uncertain about their place in the world.

Despite these challenges, men need to take the time to reflect on their values, beliefs, and aspirations and to align their actions with the legacy they wish to leave behind. Defining your personal legacy requires careful planning and foresight, a willingness to confront the unknown and navigate through the uncertainties of life. By cultivating self-awareness and prioritizing introspection, men can work toward leaving a meaningful, purposeful, and authentic legacy.

So, how do you start determining your personal legacy?

- By slowing down to consider the direction you want to take in life
- By clarifying your values, principles, and beliefs
- By aligning your goals with your purpose in life
- By determining what mark, you want to leave in the world

By embracing vulnerability, cultivating self-awareness, and prioritizing introspection, men can uncover their true purpose and define an authentic, meaningful, and enduring legacy. It's not about the size of your impact but the depth of the imprint you leave on the world and the lives of those around you.

Combatting The Fear of Insignificance

The fear of insignificance is a formidable foe that can hold men back from realizing their true potential. It weighs heavily on the hearts of many men, a shadow lurking in the recesses of their minds, casting doubt on their worth and purpose. The thought of living a life that fades into obscurity, devoid of meaning or impact, is enough to send shivers down the spine. It's a universal concern that transcends age, culture, and background, rooted in the innate desire to leave a mark on the world, to be remembered long after we're gone.

This fear, however, is not without merit. In a world that often measures success by external markers such as wealth, status, and recognition, it's easy to feel small and insignificant in comparison. Men, in particular, may feel the weight of societal expectations bearing down on their shoulders, driving them to prove their worth through tangible achievements and accomplishments.

Your value in this world isn't measured by the number of trophies on a shelf or the size of a bank account. It lies in the impact we have on the lives of others and the lasting impression we leave on the world around us. It's about shifting the focus from external validation to internal fulfillment, from seeking approval to embracing authenticity. It's about recognizing that true significance stems not from what we do but from who we are and how we choose to show up in the world.

Are you showing up the way you want in the world?

How To Overcome Your Fears

Do you ever feel insignificant? At its core, the fear of insignificance stems from a belief that our actions are inconsequential. It's a whisper in the back of our minds, telling us that we're not enough, that our dreams are too big, and our ambitions too lofty. But the truth is far different. Every action, no matter how small, has the potential to create a ripple effect, echoing through the corridors of time and shaping the course of history.

To overcome the fear of insignificance, we must first understand its origins. Perhaps it stems from childhood insecurities or past failures, lingering like ghosts in the shadows of our sub-conscious. Or it could be fueled by societal pressures and unre-alistic expectations, perpetuated by a culture that values suc-cess above all else. Whatever its source, recognizing the roots of our fear is the first step toward liberation.

- Acknowledge and confront it head-on. By acknowledging our fears and vulnerabilities, we reclaim power over them and no longer allow them to dictate our lives
- Shift your mindset to create a feeling of abundance and significance
- Seek support from others
- Take action

Once you acknowledge and confront your fears, you can work on changing your perceptions. Start by cultivating a mind-set of abundance rather than scarcity. Instead of viewing the world through a lens of limitation, we must recognize the oppor-tunities surrounding us. Every interaction presents a chance to make a difference and leave a positive imprint on the world. Next, reframe your perception of yourself and your place in the world. Instead of dwelling on our perceived shortcomings, we must focus on our inherent significance, on the gifts and talents that make us unique. We can find our inherent worth by embrac-ing our strengths and celebrating our achievements, no matter how small.

Overcoming the fear of insignificance is not a solo journey; it requires the support and encouragement of others. Surround yourself with individuals who believe in your potential and inspire you to reach for the stars. Seek mentors and role models who have walked the path before you and can offer guidance and wisdom as you navigate life's challenges.

Take action. Break free from fear and uncertainty to pursue your passions with courage and conviction. Whether starting a new business, pursuing a creative endeavor, or volunteering in your community, every step you take toward your goals is a victory in the battle against insignificance. Embrace the power of even the smallest actions to make a meaningful impact on the world around you.

While the world may celebrate the achievements of the rich and famous, true significance often lies in the small, everyday moments that go unnoticed. A kind word, a helping hand, a listening ear — these simple acts of kindness have the power to ripple outwards, touching lives in ways we may never fully comprehend.

By embracing our inherent value, we can break free from the shackles of insignificance and step into our full potential as agents of positive change. The world is waiting for you to shine your light brightly and leave your mark on the tapestry of existence.

Passing on Wisdom and Values

Have you ever been mentored by someone? Have you ever taken the time to pass your wisdom and values on to a younger person?

I've come to understand there are certain lessons and wisdom that can only be imparted from one man to another. Men and women experience the world differently, so it's natural for men to seek guidance from other men. The absence of male mentors can subtly impact a man's overall development.

Mentors offer more than just guidance; they broaden one's understanding of what it means to be a man. Each man has unique experiences, trials, and wisdom that can inspire, comfort, and help others become better men.

In a recent discussion, Jason, a middle-aged father, told me about a mentor relationship that he developed with a young man named Steve in his small group at church. Steve was struggling with direction in his life, and this group was the perfect place to share his dilemmas.

Steve was dealing with career uncertainty and relationship challenges. Jason, known for his wisdom and humility, naturally took on a mentoring role. During group discussions, Jason listened intently, offering advice rooted in his own life experiences and biblical teachings. He didn't impose his views but guided Steve to reflect on his values, faith, and the kind of life he wanted to build.

Over time, their relationship grew outside the small group. They met for coffee, talked through tough decisions, and prayed together. Jason encouraged Steve to pursue his passions and reminded him of the importance of integrity, both in his personal and professional life. He also modeled how to balance work, faith, and family, showing Steve that it was possible to live a fulfilling, purpose-driven life.

I've heard stories like this over and over again, and I have experienced them for myself. At its core, mentoring is about more than just imparting knowledge; it's about building relationships, fostering growth, and instilling values that transcend generations. The act of mentoring is a profound expression of humanity's collective wisdom and compassion. It ensures that our legacy lives on long after we're gone.

If we fail to mentor future generations, we are doing a disservice to others and society as a whole. However, in the rush of daily life, it's easy to overlook the importance of mentorship and its role in shaping the values and beliefs of our children and grandchildren.

Mentoring is a universal principle that transcends boundaries, connecting us in a shared journey of growth and discovery.

People of any age, gender, or background can be mentors. It is a sacred tradition that bridges the gap between past, present, and future.

As a mentor, you have a lot to offer others. With your help, younger generations can learn values like integrity, resilience, and perseverance. Your influence has the power to profoundly shape their lives.

Here are some of the benefits of mentoring:

- It allows you to share invaluable insights gained from your own experiences.
- It helps foster growth and nurture potential in others.
- It provides younger people with the support and guidance to navigate life's challenges confidently and resiliently.
- It allows both mentor and mentee to gain fresh perspectives and a renewed sense of purpose.
- It enriches the lives of both the mentor and mentee.

So, how can you offer your wisdom to others? It could be through formal mentorship programs, informal gatherings, or simple acts of kindness and guidance. It can be as simple as listening, sharing our experiences, and offering advice and support when needed. You could also form an apprenticeship where you teach a trade or other practical career skills that will serve them well professionally. You can help counsel a younger man with difficulty in his marriage or other relationships. No matter what, your mentorship leaves an indelible mark on the world.

Perhaps mentoring's most profound impact lies in its ability to shape the values and perspectives of others. In a world where integrity, empathy, and compassion are increasingly rare commodities, mentoring offers a beacon of hope — a chance to instill in others the timeless principles that have guided humanity for centuries. So, embrace the art of mentoring, and let your legacy be one of wisdom, compassion, and positive change.

Are you passing down your wisdom and knowledge?

Building Your Community

When considering your legacy, let us remember the communities we serve. In the context of this book, when I refer to "community," I am referring to your neighborhood or city, as well as the organizations or groups you encounter. These are the places where you can build a lasting legacy.

In an age where personal success often takes center stage, community impact is often overlooked. Yet, in this increasingly interconnected world, the ripple effect of our actions within our communities resonates far beyond our own lives. By narrowing our focus solely on personal success, we limit our potential for growth and contribution, depriving ourselves of the richness that comes from meaningful connections and shared experiences. Men need to recognize the immense potential for positive change that lies within their grasp.

Why invest in your community?

- It provides you with the profound satisfaction of contributing to a collective purpose.
- Connecting with others provides personal satisfaction and other health benefits.
- It allows you to make a tangible difference in the lives of others.
- It allows you to leverage your skills, resources, and influence.
- It allows us to grow personally and professionally
- Fostering a sense of community responsibility enriches our lives and cultivates a culture of collaboration, empathy, and resilience.

How are you connecting with others to benefit the communities you're involved in?

We must recognize that there is a symbiotic relationship between personal success and community well-being. When our communities thrive, so do we, and vice versa. It's about stepping up to the plate, taking ownership of our communities' challenges, and working together to find solutions. Whether volunteering your time, sharing your expertise, or advocating for social change, every contribution, no matter how small, has the power to make a difference.

Uncovering the transformative power of actively engaging with your community is more than just a noble pursuit; it's a journey of self-discovery and empowerment that has the potential to shape both your personal growth and the well-being of the collective. This section serves as a beacon, illuminating the reciprocal relationship between a flourishing individual and community impact, demonstrating how each enriches the other.

Community involvement is not just about giving; it's also about receiving. By immersing yourself in the rich tapestry of community life, you'll gain valuable insights, forge lasting friendships, and cultivate a sense of connection and purpose that enhances every aspect of your life.

How are you stepping outside of your comfort zone to engage with people?

You'll learn how to contribute meaningfully to your community through real-life examples and practical strategies. No matter your background or skill set, there are countless ways to make a difference in your community. It could be through volunteering, civic engagement, or grassroots initiatives. Here are some examples:

- Organize neighborhood clean-ups
- Volunteer for your church's homeless outreach programs
- Donate blood
- Mow an elderly neighbor's lawn
- Collect and donate school supplies or backpacks
- Volunteer as a school crossing guard
- Collect and donate food to a local food pantry
- Volunteer at an animal shelter
- Coach a youth sports team
- Help your neighbors with repairs[46]

Whether attending community events, joining clubs or organizations, or simply striking up conversations with your neighbors, each interaction can enrich your life in ways you never imagined.

By stepping outside your comfort zone and engaging with individuals from diverse backgrounds and perspectives, you'll broaden your horizons, expand your understanding of the world, and develop valuable skills such as communication, leadership, and empathy. These experiences enhance your life and empower you to become a more effective agent of change in your community and beyond.

So, let this section be your guide as you embark on this transformative journey toward creating a legacy of connection, compassion, and positive change in your community.

Summary of Legacy Impact

This chapter underscores the significance of men leaving a meaningful legacy, providing practical guidance to create a lasting impact. It emphasizes the importance of crafting a compelling long-term vision, actively engaging with the community, and passing on valuable wisdom. Each solution addresses a crucial

---

[46] For more community service ideas, check out https://dosomething.org/article/community-service-project-ideas

aspect of destination legacy and impact, empowering men to make a difference in their own lives and the world around them. As you embark on this journey, remember that your actions hold the power to shape not only your future but also the broader narrative of the world you live in.

Scan the code above with your smartphone
to view my chapter wrap-up video.

Go to this link to access the Chapter Worksheets:
https://truemanlifecoaching.com/TrueManTrueWaysWorksheets

Rest Stop

**Journal and reflect on your thoughts about having
a legacy and impact and how it can move you
toward becoming the True Man you want to be.**

_____

_____

_____

_____

_____

_____

_____

_____

_____

_____

_____

_____

_____

_____

_____

_____

_____

_____

_____

TRUE MAN

Epilogue

Post-Road Trip Checklist

True Man Tip

A good road trip with friends or family can create a lifetime of memories. There is a 100% chance of consequences for all of your actions while you are on it. You get to pick the action, so choose wisely.

Just as we started our road trip to the masculine heart with a car checklist, we should end with one because maintaining your car after a long journey is crucial for optimal performance.

Check tire pressure. Even though you checked it before hitting the road, it is essential to do it again upon your return. Tire pressure fluctuates with temperature changes, affecting performance and fuel efficiency. Ensure your tires are properly inflated for optimal performance.

Rotate tires. Driving adds wear and tear to your tires. Regular tire rotation is essential to maintain even wear. Rotate them before and after long trips. The timing of the rotation upon return depends on the mileage covered.

Check or change oil. Long road trips take a toll on your vehicle. Check oil levels before, during, and after the trip to ensure optimal performance. If you've exceeded the recommended mileage, consider an oil change upon your return.

Clean inside and out. Don't let dirt accumulate on your car. Remove the debris and bugs promptly to prevent exterior damage. Grime can harm your car's paint over time. Similarly, clean the interior to prevent odors and preserve upholstery.

Regular post-road trip maintenance ensures your car stays in prime condition for future journeys.

Now that we have taken care of the car, what about you?

Take care of your heart.

Your heart is much like your car; ignoring the warning signs can get you into real trouble, and everything can spin into chaos. Take time to check in with yourself to see if everything is in order. It's not just about ticking off boxes on a self-help checklist; it's about embracing a holistic and faith-filled approach to life that empowers you to thrive in every aspect.

Pay attention to your mental and emotional needs.

Neglecting your mental health needs can cause engine failure because it leaves you vulnerable to stress, anxiety, and depression. If you ignore your emotional well-being, you can become disconnected from yourself and those around you. This also leads to other problems in your career and relationships.

Get physically fit.

Disregarding your body's needs leads to disease and deterioration. Think of your physical body as if it were a chassis: When you fail to care for it, it crumbles. Poor health choices, like a sedentary lifestyle and unhealthy eating habits, pave the way for chronic illnesses that sap your energy and vitality. Living a healthier lifestyle gives you the strength and stamina needed to fully engage in your life.

Get right with God.

Spiritual neglect manifests as a lack of exposure to spiritual concepts and growth opportunities. Nurturing spiritual growth gives you a sense of purpose and helps you navigate the road of life with resilience and grace.

Get in touch with your authentic self.

Putting a new coat of paint on an old Buick doesn't turn it into a Porsche. Likewise, masking your vulnerability can leave you isolated and alone. However, being honest with the people in your life can heal relationships. Permitting your authentic self to shine through allows you to forge the genuine connections you want.

Find direction in your life by creating actionable goals.

What is your purpose in life? Take the time to figure out your passions and goals, then write down what you want to accomplish and the steps needed to get there. Once you have a map, you'll be able to reach your potential and make a positive impact on the world.

Build a solid financial foundation.

Financial instability creates a constant undercurrent of stress and uncertainty. Provide for yourself and your family by making good decisions like reducing debt and budgeting,

Cultivate a lasting legacy.

Consider what mark you want to leave on the world and build your legacy from there. True fulfillment comes from creating a positive impact and inspiring others to do the same.

To truly thrive, a man must prioritize his emotional, physical, and spiritual well-being, nurture authentic relationships, set meaningful goals, and leave a lasting legacy that echoes through the ages.

Becoming a True Man is about living with passion and purpose. The Apostle Paul proclaimed that through Christ, he and all believers are endowed with God's righteousness. Driven by the boundless value of knowing Christ, Paul dedicated his life to deepening his relationship with the Savior. This pursuit was his ultimate purpose and passion, shaping every action and guiding every individual he led.

Philippians 3: 7-9 (KJV) exudes Paul's confidence when he writes,

"But what things were gain to me, those I counted loss for Christ. Yea doubtless, and I count all things but loss for Christ. Yea doubtless, and I count all things but loss for the excellency of the knowledge of Christ Jesus my Lord: for who I have suffered the loss of all things and do count them but dung that I may win Christ. And be found in him, not having mine own righteousness, which is of the law, but that which is through the faith of Christ, the righteousness which is of God by faith."

I hope you follow Paul's passion and Christ's path as you begin planning for your life and legacy. Jesus' last recorded words in scripture came on the cross as He died, "And when Jesus had cried with a loud voice, he said, Father, into thy hands I commend my spirit: and having said thus, he gave up the ghost." Luke 24:46 (KJV)

May the Spirit of God reign over you as you discover His grace and mercy, discover your heart, and become the True Man you were meant to be.

Scan the code above with your smartphone
to view my book wrap-up video.

Bibliography

"12 Gratitude Journal Prompts to Add to Your Self-Care Routine." Web log. *Calm* (blog). Calm. Accessed August 8, 2024. https://www.calm.com/blog/gratitude-journal-prompts.

Alshami, Ali M. "Pain: Is It All in the Brain or the Heart?" *Current pain and headache reports* vol. 23,12 88. 14 Nov. 2019, doi:10.1007/s11916-019-0827-4

badgesforall. "The History of Journaling and Famous Journals." Web log. *Badges for All* (blog). Badges for All, January 8, 2020. https://badgesforall.wordpress.com/2020/01/08/the-history-of-journaling-and-famous-journals/.

Blake, Suzanne. "Rising Number of Men Don't Want to Work." *Newsweek.* May 6, 2024. https://www.newsweek.com/american-men-dont-want-work-anymore-1897567.

Brown, Shelby. "Where Did Writing Come From?" Getty News. Getty Museum, April 27, 2021. https://www.getty.edu/news/where-did-writing-come-from/.

Byock, Ira. The four things that matter most: Essential wisdom for transforming your relationships and your life. New York: Free Press, 2004.

Canfield, Jack. "Taking 100% Responsibility for Your Life." Web log. *Jackcanfield.Com* (blog). Jack Canfield. Accessed August 8, 2024. https://jackcanfield.com/blog/taking-100-responsibility-for-your-life/.

Capua, Rebecca. "Papyrus-Making in Egypt: Essay: The Metropolitan Museum of Art: Heilbrunn Timeline of Art History." Papyrus-Making in Egypt, March 2015. https://www.metmuseum.org/toah/hd/pyma/hd_pyma.htm.

Coughlin, Steven S. "Post-traumatic Stress Disorder and Cardiovascular Disease." *The open cardiovascular medicine journal* vol. 5 (2011): 164-70. doi:10.2174/1874192401105010164

Courtney E. Ackerman, MA. "Benefits of Gratitude: 28+ Surprising Research Findings." PositivePsychology.com, June 26, 2024. https://positivepsychology.com/benefits-gratitude-research-questions/.

Cox, Daniel A. "The State of American Friendship: Change, Challenges, and Loss." American Survey Center, June 8, 2021. https://www.americansurveycenter.org/research/the-state-of-american-friendship-change-challenges-and-loss/.

Department of Health & Human Services. "Physical Activity - How to Get Active When You Are Busy." Better Health Channel, January 10, 2017. https://www.betterhealth.vic.gov.au/health/healthyliving/Physical-activity-how-to-get-active-when-you-are-busy.

Ellingson, Laura D et al. "Changes in sedentary time are associated with changes in mental wellbeing over 1 year in young adults." *Preventive medicine reports* vol. 11 274-281. 30 Jul. 2018, doi: 10.1016/j.pmedr.2018.07.013

Flegal, Katherine M. "Prevalence and Trends in Obesity among US Adults, 1999-2008." *JAMA* 303, no. 3 (January 20, 2010): 235–41. https://doi.org/10.1001/jama.2009.2014.

"Functions of Blood: Transport around the Body." NHS Blood Donation. Accessed August 8, 2024. https://www.blood.co.uk/news-and-campaigns/the-donor/latest-stories/functions-of-blood-transport-around-the-body/.

Goldman, Erik. "The Obesity Epidemic: It's a Guy Thing." Holistic Primary Care, October 30, 2013. https://holisticprimarycare.net/topics/chronic-disease/the-obesity-epidemic-its-a-guy-thing-2/.

"Horsepower." Wikipedia, June 29, 2024.
https://en.wikipedia.org/wiki/Horsepower.

Horton, Cassidy. "The Silent Strain: How Debt Takes a Toll
on Mental Health." Edited by Michael Benninger. Forbes,
October 2, 2023. https://www.forbes.com/advisor/banking/
american-debt-and-the-mental-health-epidemic/.

Jiménez, Gina. "Slipping on Your New Year's Resolutions? Science
Tips to Get on Track." *Scientific American*. Scientific American,
January 22, 2024. https://www.scientificamerican.com/article/
slipping-on-your-new-years-resolutions-science-tips-to-get-on-track/.

Knight, Rebecca. "8 Essential Qualities of Successful
Leaders." *Harvard Business Review*. Harvard
Business Review, December 13, 2023. https://hbr.
org/2023/12/8-essential-qualities-of-successful-leaders.

Lachance, Laura, and Drew Ramsey. "Food, mood, and brain health:
implications for the modern clinician." *Missouri medicine* vol. 112,2
(2015): 111-5.

LaMotte, Sandee. "Ultraprocessed Foods Linked to Heart Disease,
Diabetes, Mental Disorders and Early Death, Study Finds."
CNN. February 28, 2024. https://www.cnn.com/2024/02/28/
health/ultraprocessed-food-health-risks-study-wellness/index.
html#:~:text=%E2%80%9

Maxwell, John C. The power of significance: How purpose changes
your life. New York: Center Street, 2017.
https://www.amazon.com/Power-Significance-Purpose-Changes-Your/
dp/1455548219

Medical News Today. "Why Is Sleep Important? 9 Reasons for
Getting a Good Night's Rest." Medical News Today. Accessed August
11, 2024. https://www.medicalnewstoday.com/articles/325353.

Movember: Changing the Face of Men's Health! GatorCare, November 1, 2022. https://gatorcare.org/2022/11/01/movember-changing-the-face-of-mens health/#:~:text=Men%20are%204%20times%20more,hesitate%20to%20ask%20for%20help.

Nadinloyi, Karim Babayi, Hasan Sadeghi, and Nader Hajloo. "Relationship between Job Satisfaction and Employees Mental Health." Procedia - Social and Behavioral Sciences 84 (July 2013): 293–97. https://doi.org/10.1016/j.sbspro.2013.06.554.

Office of the Surgeon General (OSG). Our Epidemic of Loneliness and Isolation: The U.S. Surgeon General's Advisory on the Healing Effects of Social Connection and Community. US Department of Health and Human Services, 2023.

"Parchment." In Encyclopedia Britannica. Accessed August 8, 2024. https://www.britannica.com/topic/parchment.

Park, Jung Ha et al. "Sedentary Lifestyle: Overview of Updated Evidence of Potential Health Risks." Korean journal of family medicine vol. 41,6 (2020): 365-373. doi:10.4082/kjfm.20.0165

Prakash, Prarthana. "Men Are Dropping out of the Labor Force Because They're Upset about Their Social Status, According to a New Study." Fortune. Fortune, December 7, 2022. https://fortune.com/2022/12/07/men-dropping-out-work-force-status-study/amp/

Rafique, Nazish et al. "Effects of Mobile Use on Subjective Sleep Quality." Nature and science of sleep vol. 12 357-364. 23 June. 2020, doi:10.2147/NSS.S253375

Raypole, Crystal. "Ready, Set, Journal! 64 Journaling Prompts for Self-Discovery." Psych Central, May 17, 2021. https://psychcentral.com/blog/ready-set-journal-64-journaling-prompts-for-self-discovery.

"Risks of Physical Inactivity." Johns Hopkins Medicine, March 4, 2024. https://www.hopkinsmedicine.org/health/conditions-and-diseases/risks-of-physical-inactivity.

Sagar-Ouriaghli, Ilyas et al. "Improving Mental Health Service Utilization Among Men: A Systematic Review and Synthesis of Behavior Change Techniques Within Interventions Targeting Help-Seeking." *American journal of men's health* vol. 13,3 (2019): 1557988319857009. doi:10.1177/1557988319857009

Schwartz, Daniel. "Suicide Rates Are Highest for Men in Their 50s and We're Not Sure Why." https://www.cbc.ca/news/health/suicide-men-50s-causes-1.3263412*CBC News*. November 6, 2015.

"Study Focuses on Strategies for Achieving Goals, Resolutions." *Dominican.Edu*. Dominican University of California, February 1, 2015. Dominican University of California. https://scholar.dominican.edu/cgi/viewcontent.cgi?article=1265&context=news-releases.

Terlizzi, Emily P. and Zablotsky, Benjamin. "Mental Health Treatment Among Adults: United States, 2019." CDC.gov. CDC, September 2020. Accessed August 8, 2024. https://www.cdc.gov/nchs/products/databriefs/db380.htm

Witters, Dan. "Loneliness in U.S. Subsides from Pandemic High." Gallup.com, February 7, 2024. https://news.gallup.com/poll/473057/loneliness-subsides-pandemic-high.aspx.

Wu, Xiu Yun et al. "The influence of physical activity, sedentary behavior on health-related quality of life among the general population of children and adolescents: A systematic review." *PloS one* vol. 12,11 e0187668. 9 Nov. 2017, doi:10.1371/journal.pone.0187668

About the Author

Mike Van Pelt is a seasoned Christian men's coach, dedicated to helping men uncover their true potential, build stronger character, and create lasting legacies. With years of experience in leadership, personal development, and coaching, Mike has impacted countless lives by inspiring men to pursue purpose over mediocrity and integrity over complacency. He is the founder of True Man Life Coaching a community focused on the radical reconstruction of a man's heart and soul, empowering men to embrace authentic masculinity in every role they take on — be it husband, father, leader, or friend.

Through his work, Mike brings a straightforward, no-nonsense approach to personal growth, combining faith-based principles with actionable strategies for success. He's also the creator of the *True Man Podcast*, where he explores what it means to live as a true man, leading with purpose, passion, and unwavering commitment to moving towards success. In addition, Mike is an entrepreneur, three-time international best-selling author, and speaker. He is also the Vice President of Givers University® USA Campuses and a member of the Givers University® Board of Regents.

When he isn't coaching, Mike is pursuing his purpose as a devoted husband and father, seeking to inspire the next generation to live with boldness, resilience, and godly integrity.

Connect with Mike:

https://truemanlifecoaching.com
https://truemanpodcast.com/
https://www.facebook.com/CoachMikeVanPelt/
https://x.com/truemancoaching
https://www.instagram.com/truemancoaching/
https://www.linkedin.com/in/mikevanpelt/
https://www.youtube.com/@truemanpodcast

Have You Enjoyed This Book?

We invite you to post a review:

And we would be pleased if you would
share this book with others that you know will benefit:

www.ingramcontent.com/pod-product-compliance
Lightning Source LLC
Chambersburg PA
CBHW051137120626
46547CB00012B/844